Hegel and the French Revolution

Studies in Contemporary German Social Thought
Thomas McCarthy, general editor

Alfred Schmidt, *History and Structure: An Essay on Hegelian-Marxist and Structuralist Theories of History*, 1981

Hans-Georg Gadamer, *Reason in the Age of Science*, 1982

Joachim Ritter, *Hegel and the French Revolution: Essays on the Philosophy of Right*, 1982

Theodor W. Adorno, *Prisms*, 1982

Hegel and the French Revolution

Essays on the *Philosophy of Right*

Joachim Ritter
Translated with an Introduction by
Richard Dien Winfield

The MIT Press
Cambridge, Massachusetts
London, England

First paperback printing, 1984

© 1982 by
The Massachusetts Institute of Technology

This translation © 1982 by the Massachusetts Institute of Technology. These essays originally appeared in German as part of Ritter's book *Metaphysik und Politik: Studien zu Aristoteles und Hegel,* © 1969 by Suhrkamp Verlag, Frankfurt, Federal Republic of Germany.

This book was set in Baskerville by Graphic Composition, Inc., and printed and bound by The Murray Printing Co. in the United States of America.

Library of Congress Cataloging in Publication Data

Ritter, Joachim, 1903–1974.
  Hegel and the French Revolution.

  (Studies in contemporary German social thought)
  1. Hegel, Georg Wilhelm Friedrich, 1770–1831—Addresses, essays, lectures.
2. France—History—Revolution, 1789–1799—Addresses, essays, lectures.
3. Hegel, Georg Wilhelm Friedrich, 1770–1831. Grundlinien der Philosophie des Rechts—Addresses, essays, lectures. 4. Law—Philosophy—Addresses, essays, lectures. 5. Political science—Addresses, essays, lectures. 6. Natural law—Addresses, essays, lectures. 7. Ethics—Addresses, essays, lectures. I. Title.
II. Series.
B2948.R57   172   82–55
ISBN 0–262–18105–3 AACR2

Contents

Contents

Series Foreword

From Hegel and Marx, Dilthey and Weber, to Freud and the Frankfurt School, German social theory enjoyed an undisputed preeminence. After the violent break brought about by National Socialism and World War II, this tradition has recently come to life again, and indeed to such an extent that contemporary German social thought has begun to approach the heights earlier attained. One important element in this renaissance has been the rapid and extensive translation into German of English-language works in the humanities and the social sciences, with the result that social thought in Germany is today markedly influenced by ideas and approaches of Anglo-American origin. Unfortunately, efforts in the other direction, the translation and reception of German works into English, have been sporadic at best. This series is intended to correct that imbalance.

The term *social thought* is here understood very broadly to include not only sociological and political thought as such but also the social-theoretical concerns of history and philosophy, psychology and linguistics, aesthetics and theology. The term *contemporary* is also to be construed broadly: though our attention will be focused primarily on postwar thinkers, we shall also publish works by and on earlier thinkers whose influence on contemporary German social thought is pervasive. The series will begin with translations of works by authors whose names are already widely recognized in English-speaking countries—Adorno, Bloch, Gadamer, Habermas, Marcuse, Ritter—and by authors of similar accomplishment who are not yet so familiar outside of Germany—Blumenberg, Peukert, Schmidt, Theunissen, Tugendhat. Subsequent volumes will also include monographs and collections of essays written in English on German social thought and its concerns.

To understand and appropriate other traditions is to broaden the horizons of one's own. It is our hope that this series, by tapping a neglected store of intellectual riches and making it accessible to the English-speaking public, will expand the frame of reference of our social and political discourse.

Thomas McCarthy

A Note on the Translation

The translations of several key terms of Hegel to which Ritter frequently refers require some explanation.

Central among these terms is *Recht*, which is commonly used to designate right, justice, or law. Hegel himself specifically defines it as the determinate being of freedom, and I have accordingly translated *Recht* as "right" whenever this meaning is intended.

In German philosophy preceding Hegel, *Privatrecht* signified natural right in contrast to *bürgerliches Recht*, which designated the public right of civil government. With Hegel these terms take on a very different meaning requiring an alternate translation. When Ritter refers to *Privatrecht* in Hegel, what he is designating is not natural right but the non-natural *abstract right* enjoyed by persons in their property relations with one another and posited in legal form within civil law. On the other hand, Hegel uses *bürgerliches Recht* to designate the determinate being of freedom within civil society. The latter is not a civil government devoted to enforcing natural right, but a society separate from the state and containing within its subordinate social sphere the economy, the administration of civil law and public welfare, and social interest groups. At times Hegel does use *bürgerliches Recht* in the narrow sense of civil law. When this usage appears in Ritter's discussion it is translated as "civil law," whereas whenever *bürgerliches Recht* figures as the freedom of civil society in general, it is translated as "civil right."

A related translation difficulty arises in Hegel's usage of *Ding* and *Sache*, terms frequently cited by Ritter, who further draws the distinction between *Verdinglichung* and *Versachlichung*. Although *Ding* and *Sache* are not consistently distinguished in T. M. Knox's standard translation of the *Philosophy of Right*, Hegel gives them very different technical meanings which he rigorously maintains. Hegel indicates their general distinction in his *Logic*. There *Ding* appears within the "Logic of Essence" as an entity standing relative to others within the causal relations of existence. *Sache*, on the other hand, is introduced within the "Logic of The Concept" as an entity which does not stand under an external necessity, but rather exhibits self-determination, the freedom of the concept, in an objective embodiment. In the *Philosophy of Right*, *Sache* more specifically refers to an entity which can embody the self-determination of the will of a person by becoming his recognized property. As Ritter notes (see page 132 following), Hegel argues that not all *Dingen* can become *Sachen* since some, like the sun and stars, cannot be taken possession of in a recognizable way. *Versachlichung* and *Verdinglichung* thus connote very different processes, the former designating the process whereby external entities become property, the medium in which persons give their freedom a recognized existence, and the latter designating the process whereby what is not a mere thing becomes treated as one. To maintain these important distinctions, I have translated *Ding* as "thing" and *Sache* as "object of the will." The use of "object of the will" for *Sache* seems more appropriate here than the term "fact" which A. V. Miller uses for *Sache* in his translation of the *Science of Logic*. I have accordingly translated *Verdinglichung* as "reification," and *Versachlichung* as "determination as object of the will," "mediation through objects of the will," or "determination of objects of the will," depending upon the context.

Nevertheless, for the sake of simplicity, all citations from and page and paragraph references to the *Philosophy of Right* have been taken from T. M. Knox's translation, published by Oxford University Press, New York, 1967, except when they refer to Hegel's own marginal notes which appear only in the indicated German edition.

Works frequently referred to in the text have been cited using the abbreviations listed below, followed by the volume number in Roman numerals and the page number in Arabic numerals. All other works are cited in the text, following their first citation, with the author's last name, followed by the page numbers in question.

List of Abbreviations

Br.
Briefe von und an Hegel, Hoffmeister Edition.

DFS
G. W. F. Hegel, *The Difference Between Fichte's and Schelling's System of Philosophy*, Albany, 1977.

DV
I. Kant, *Doctrine of Virtue*, Philadelphia, 1964.

FK
G. W. F. Hegel, *Faith and Knowledge*, Albany, 1977.

HPW
Hegel's Political Writings, Oxford, 1964.

LHP

G. W. F. Hegel, *Lectures on the History of Philosophy*, New York, 1968.

MEJ

I. Kant, *The Metaphysical Elements of Justice*, Indianapolis, 1978.

PH

G. W. F. Hegel, *Philosophy of History*, New York, 1956.

PR

G. W. F. Hegel, *Philosophy of Right*, New York, 1967.

PS

G. W. F. Hegel, *Phenomenology of Spirit*, New York, 1977.

SL

G. W. F. Hegel, *Science of Logic*, New York, 1969.

Last, I would like to thank Thomas McCarthy for his very careful editing of this translation and for his many suggestions that have been incorporated for its improvement.

Richard Dien Winfield

Hegel and the French Revolution

Translator's Introduction

Ever since Hegel's death his philosophy of right has been the subject of incessant, often vehement debate, impelled by an awareness that at issue are the problems most central to modernity. Unfortunately, the discussion has generally been restricted to establishing whether Hegel's theory of right provides insight into the structure of the modern world, in order then to celebrate or condemn his thought as progressive or reactionary.

For all the literature it has generated, this prevailing interpretative approach has rested on an unexamined premise that has made it blind to Hegel's own fundamental concerns. Unlike the work it criticizes, it assumes that one can directly refer to our own age as a criterion by which to judge conceptions of right, and so speak of what is "progressive" and "just" in one and the same breath. It fails to recognize that whether or not Hegel's philosophy of right corresponds with modern reality has no normative theoretical or practical significance unless it has already been established that modern relations are intrinsically just. They are not given facts of nature, subject to laws independent of our wills, but historically emergent structures susceptible of practical critique and alteration. Consequently, a discrepancy between a theory of right and existing institutions may require not a revolution in science, but one in reality instead.

Hegel is aware of this in the most uncompromising way. He not only rejects any prescriptive role for historically given institutions, but demands that the structures of right be conceived without any constitutive reference to what one already "finds" in reality.[1] He recognizes that if the theory of justice were to rely upon such immediate givens for its content, it would be doubly at fault: both in claiming normative validity for what is only a particular circumstance, and in committing the basic metaphysical error of assuming the correspondence of its thought with reality by directly asserting the truth of what it finds given.

Accordingly, for Hegel the legitimacy of modernity cannot be taken for granted, but is rather a very real problem which must be addressed *within* philosophical science from the vantage point of the theory of justice. Few interpreters have heeded this point, and consequently there has been little effort to come to grips with the actual arguments that give Hegel's philosophy of right its seminal importance and special role in the evaluation of modernity.

Joachim Ritter is an exception to the rule. In his essays on Hegel's practical philosophy, Ritter has done us the service of calling attention to Hegel's understanding of modernity by focusing upon the central problems of right with which Hegel is concerned. This is not an achievement of merely scholarly import, for what Ritter sets in relief in Hegel's philosophy of right are the basic conceptual tools for assessing the justice of the modern age and developing further the theory of justice itself.

At the heart of the matter is Hegel's concept of freedom; for, as Ritter makes clear, Hegel's theory of justice is more radically a theory of freedom than any other. What immediately sets Hegel's philosophy of right apart is that it is devoted to establishing and determining justice as freedom, not by postulating freedom as the prior principle of justice, but by developing the structures of justice themselves as the constitutive reality of freedom.

In contrast to liberal theory, Hegel does not proceed from any predetermined notion of freedom, which is then employed as a principle to determine and legitimate the various relations of right. Hegel recognizes that such an endeavor is inherently aporetic for the simple reason that taking the free will as a principle robs it and the justice derived from it of all actual freedom. The moment one treats freedom as a principle, it is reduced to something whose character is given prior to what it determines. Consequently, the free will does not determine itself in the structures of justice derived from it, for it does not give itself any further content in them, but rather determines, as a principle, what is secondary to and other than it. Conversely, the derivative relations of right are not self-determined structures themselves, for they are determined by what is given prior to and separately from them. What results is a freedom with no objective reality and a system of justice unable to exhibit the very principle which can alone legitimate it.

Hegel avoids this dilemma from the very start by conceiving right as the Idea of freedom, that is, as the system of justice consisting in the relations in which the free will determines itself in all its possible modes and thereby achieves its full realization. As Ritter points out, Hegel expressly declares that the philosophy of right can have no other task than following out the self-determination of the Idea of freedom, and it is on this basis and this basis alone that Hegel confronts the legitimacy of modernity. Three major arguments are here entailed, arguments to which Ritter draws attention in each of his essays. These can be briefly indicated in the form of three theses concerning the character of freedom.

Hegel's Three Basic Theses on Freedom

1. First of all, freedom is the sole substance and content of justice. Nothing else can provide normative validity for action. He-

gel seeks to establish this with a two-fold argument that is both negative and positive in character.

On the one hand, he attempts to show that conduct which is not self-determined, but given its character independently of free willing, can have no unconditioned universality. In contrast to freedom, such action is, as Hegel generically describes it, *naturally* determined; and insofar as it depends on something other for its essence, it cannot be an end in itself, as would be required for normative validity. In Hegel's view, the ethics and politics of Plato and Aristotle present the classic examples of a theory of justice based on natural determination, where conduct is valid not by being self-determined, but by embodying pre-scribed universal virtues, given means of conduct, and a fixed essence of goodness. In scattered critical remarks in the *Philoso-phy of Right*, Hegel effectively argues that such a theory cannot establish normative validity for its given standards of conduct without introducing an unconditioned agent to determine and impose them: a figure such as Aristotle's absolutely good man[2] or Plato's philosopher king,[3] whose autonomous rule contradicts the very framework of natural determination which it seeks to sanction.

On the other hand, Hegel goes beyond this critique to present a positive proof that justice cannot be anything but the realiza-tion of freedom. This proof effectively occupies his entire de-velopment of right. It consists first in the demonstration that freedom is itself a structure of justice, irreducibly entailing rights and duties which are for their own sake, and then second in the comprehensive demonstration that every normative sphere of action has its valid universality by comprising a spe-cific structure of freedom. These demonstrations are provided by the arguments supporting the second and third major theses on freedom, which distinguish Hegel's theory and provide the basis for Ritter's discussion.

The decisive second thesis, which sets Hegel apart from all preceding thinkers of freedom, can be stated as follows:

2. Freedom is neither a faculty given by nature, nor a capacity of the self, but a structure of interaction between individuals wherein the self-determination of each is constitutively related to that of others through mutual recognition and respect.

According to this claim, freedom can only be understood as an intersubjective structure in which the self-determinations of individuals stand indissolubly linked together in a reciprocal relation where each will autonomously determines itself in accord with the realization of others. On this basis, freedom is itself an existing right, whose respect is assured by its very exercise. As such, freedom is not a principle of justice, but rather an actual structure of justice itself, for it consists in a real exercise of freedom among individuals that goes hand in hand with the honored duty to respect it.

By itself, of course, this thesis says nothing concerning the specific content of the structure of interaction that is freedom, the particular rights and duties it involves, or the institutional forms entailed in its process. Nevertheless, the thesis sets the stage for an ethical evaluation of modernity by characterizing freedom, the substance of justice according to Hegel's first thesis, as something which exists not by nature or in virtue of the single self, but only through commonly enacted structures of interaction, which may or may not arise depending upon what relations individuals establish with one another.

This means that one should neither automatically recognize the authority of historically given institutions, nor be indifferent to them. If freedom is a structure of interaction, then it can come into existence and bring justice to the light of day only within history, through the establishment of certain forms of interrelated self-determination. If, however, its universally valid structures of justice are to arise within history, the bonds of natural determination, embodied in whatever past traditions and given authority contravene the interaction of freedom, must first be broken. Then a new foundation of practical relations must be undertaken, establishing the requisite structures of freedom. These two acts of liberation and constitution together comprise revolution in the true sense of the word.[4] In order for freedom's interaction to emerge, history must thus involve revolution, not in the orthodox Marxist sense of a necessary, socially conditioned seizure of state power, but in the preeminently political sense of a voluntary, unconditioned transformation of all practical bonds into relations of free interaction.

By conceiving justice as freedom, and freedom as interaction, Hegel is inexorably led to consider history as the domain in which freedom comes into being. He thereby not only finds himself forced to evaluate modernity with regard to the historical emergence of freedom, but to do so in light of the problem of conceiving how history can bring forth a revolution that establishes freedom as an existing world.

For these reasons, Ritter can rightly claim that Hegel is not only a philosopher of freedom, but the philosopher of revolution par excellence. Ritter realizes, however, that both freedom and revolution are empty words unless one confronts the *de jure* question of what are the constitutive structures of freedom which give revolution its content and legitimacy. This *de jure* question is what Hegel primarily addresses in the *Philosophy of Right*, and his answer can be schematically expressed as his third thesis on freedom:

3. The interaction of freedom is not a single interrelationship, leaving beside it institutions which are naturally determined, but a system of right incorporating all practical relations as determinations of freedom. It does this by having as its necessary and exhaustive reality the distinct structures of interaction comprising the just spheres of person and property, morality, the

family, civil society, and the state, all of which owe their existence to a world history that has its own developmental, universal character by bringing them into being.

The arguments supporting this final encompassing thesis are what alone provide the relevant yardstick with which Hegel evaluates the legitimacy of modernity, and it is to them that one must turn to judge his own theory, not as progressive or reactionary, but as a true or false account of what justice is.

Hegel's Critique of Kantian Practical Philosophy and His Resulting Move to Interaction

Although Hegel's own working out of the structures of right was accompanied and often inspired by his intense interest in the events of his day, what set him on the path of his theory of interaction were the philosophical problems he found in the leading theory of justice of the time, the practical philosophy of Immanuel Kant. The seminal importance of Hegel's critical encounter with Kant's practical philosophy is made clear by Ritter in his essay, "Morality and Ethical Life." Ritter goes so far as to suggest that Hegel's philosophy of right can be understood as a "sublation" of Kant's theory, in the dual sense of having its own framework immanently emerge from the inherent dilemmas of the Kantian position, and of superceding it by incorporating its standpoint as a subordinate element within the developed reality of freedom.

Kant's theory can play so important a role for Hegel's philosophy of right only in virtue of Kant's advance beyond the conception of freedom put forward by the classic representatives of the liberal tradition, Hobbes, Locke, and Rousseau. This advance consists in Kant's recognition that freedom cannot be conceived as liberty, that is, as a faculty of choice, free to choose among ends given independently to it. Although such liberty allows the will to be unbeholden to any particular content, since it can always choose another, it leaves the will bound in general to ends which it has not determined itself, but rather found before it. On the basis of liberty, action thus stands conditioned by whatever array of alternatives lies given before it, and therefore can never have any universal, normative validity.

Kant's entire theory of practical reason is motivated by the need to overcome this heteronomy of liberty and establish a basis for universally valid relations of justice by conceiving instead how the will can give itself an end which owes its content to the will itself.

For Hegel, the problem Kant here addresses must be resolved if there is to be any philosophy of right at all. Nevertheless, Hegel rejects the entire Kantian framework because, in thinking it through, he finds Kant's practical reason incapable of giving the will any real particular ends that do not derive from mere liberty. In Hegel's view, Kant's categorical imperative provides no more than an empty rule for judging the formal consistency of maxims of conduct whose own content is still supplied by a conditioned choice. Accordingly, it cannot serve as the basis of autonomy, as Kant would like.

What leads Hegel beyond practical reason to interaction is his insight that the free will can act on its own, independently of both inner desire and reason as well as outer circumstance, only in relation to other wills, and indeed, only by willing that relation as well.

On the one hand, in order for willing to have a particular end specific to freedom, its action must exhibit both a form common to the will in general and a content exclusively its own. A solitary will, or one dealing only with nature, cannot have this essential individuality of freedom, for its act refers only to what is not a will, against which it cannot individuate itself as a particular instance of a commonly existing structure of willing. To do so, the willing in question must rather stand in a contrastive relation to other willings, in which their dual identity and difference is a reality.

On the other hand, Hegel concludes that this relation to other wills cannot be imposed upon willing, as something independently given. If that were the case, the particularity of the will would not be self-determined, but determined in virtue of a contrastive differentiation beyond the bounds of its volition. Consequently, if the will is to be free, it must particularize itself by no less willing its relation to other wills.

These other wills, however, cannot be self-determined themselves, and so afford the necessary contrast term for the first will's individuation, unless their relation to it and other wills is also voluntarily established through their own particular self-determinations.

Therefore, Hegel reasons, for wills to particularize themselves, their self-determination must be a reciprocal interaction in which each wills its own objectification and relation to others in virtue of honoring the particular self-determination and relation to other which these wills simultaneously give themselves through the same act of mutual recognition and respect.

Through this line of argument, Hegel comes to the conclusion that freedom is not a natural endowment or a structure of the self, but an interaction of a plurality of individuals. Although the individuals involved must already possess a natural corporeal being and the subjective capacities of mind and choice (which Hegel accounts for in his theory of Subjective Spirit) to be able to recognize how others have willed, choose a particular objectification to will in respect of that of others, and finally give their self-determination a recognizable presence in the world, it is only through the enacted plural relations of their reciprocal recognition that their willing acquires the further qualities of free action and normative validity as well.

These latter aspects go together, Hegel maintains, because freedom irreducibly involves mutual respect for the contrasted self-determinations constituting its individual structure. Therefore, freedom is not a principle of justice, out of which relations of right are to be derived, but an actual structure of right, whose exercise is immediately bound up with the respect ensuring it objective reality.

As such, the basic concept of interaction is itself a specific relation of right, whose justice is the most indeterminate and abstract of all. Freedom is without further qualification the interrelationship of individuals in which each objectifies his will in a particular embodiment, whose limits accord with those that others give their own wills by respecting others' self-determinations. In this minimal interaction, the objectification of each will has no other character than that of being its own particularization, respected by others who have willed similar domains of their own. Conversely, the will of each has no other individuating feature than that of the particular embodiment it has given itself. Through it, each will is objectively free, but in an abstract manner; for although its particularity is determined by itself, it lies immediately outside the will in its willed embodiment. And this embodiment is equally indeterminate, for it is simply some external thing, figuring within the interaction as but a medium for the will's recognized self-determination. The specific natural features of this object of the will have no constitutive significance with respect to the will's particularization, for the will here wills not them, but its own objectification. Providing a receptacle for objective freedom, they are rendered mere accidents of what here stands recognized as the will's own particular domain.

What is thus entailed in the immediate concept of interaction is no universal ideal of freedom, awaiting embodiment, but rather the real relationship of persons through property, which Hegel recognizes to be the specifically abstract right of interaction's minimal reality. It accordingly builds the starting point of Hegel's theory of justice, presenting the identity of freedom and right in its most basic form. Here begins the positive sublation of the Kantian position, which finally gives Hegel the conceptual means for confronting modernity.

Person and Property and the Problem of Morality

Ritter is one of the few interpreters who appropriately emphasizes the significance of Hegel's concept of abstract right and how it is the basic structure of interaction, irreducible to no other. In his essay, "Person and Property," he dissects the elemental character of the relations of persons through property in Hegel's theory and at the same time points to the deficient abstractness that leads Hegel to develop further spheres of right as necessary components of freedom's full realization.

On the one hand, property relations are the most elementary structure of self-determination. As Ritter points out, Hegel's concept of abstract right shows that the person has no particular needs or other qualities within himself which enter into his self-determination as property-owner. Rather, what alone individuates him as a particular *person* distinct from others is the specific object in which his will has a recognized objectification. Conversely, an object is *property* not due to its useful properties or any other particular feature, but solely in virtue of being the recognized receptacle of a person's will. Consequently, Hegel turns aside the Jacobin demand for ownership of equal amounts of property, recognizing that the question of what or how much one owns may have relevance for other more concrete spheres of right, but not for property relations themselves. Abstract right mandates only that persons must have property of their own, since otherwise they have no objective self-determination. It cannot prescribe what or how much they own.

What abstract right does presuppose, however, is first, that nature and natural determination in general have lost all independent power over the will of individuals. For things to be appropriated as property, Hegel points out, they must face the individual as rightless objects, with no recognized independent spirit standing in the way of the objectification of his will. This means, as Ritter observes with one eye on modernity, that the desacralization of nature is a precondition of abstract right. In other words, the freedom of the person exists not in a state of nature, but only *historically*, where individuals have liberated themselves from the hold of nature.

On the other hand, Hegel argues individuals can only be persons if their right to determine themselves through property is not tied to any limiting conditions separate from their recognizable ability to make their wills known. It is not right to limit personhood by sex, race, class, national origin, or any other factor extraneous to the will's operation. Hegel accordingly condemns Roman law, despite its introduction of free property, because it allows only the select few to qualify as persons. Thus, the reality of abstract right presupposes not just that nature be desacralized, but also that individuals come to be recognized as bearers of a free will, irrespective of any natural determinations unrelated to the will's recognizable expression. As Ritter observes, Hegel notes that only in modern times has this precondition begun to be realized, establishing the most elemental of rights, the right to property, as a universal aspect of the life of willing individuals.

Although these preconditions render the existence of abstract right a result of specific historical developments, they are not themselves structures of justice. Accordingly, they do not displace abstract right as the starting point of the theory of right. Nevertheless, though property relations comprise the most basic interaction of freedom, Hegel recognizes that abstract right entails conflicts and wrongs that cannot be resolved and righted through its own means alone. By its very character, the reciprocal recognition determining property relations leaves it a matter of contingency what individuals happen to choose as the object of their will and what they thereby decide to acknowledge as the domain of others. Therefore, it is always possible for persons to enter into conflicts of non-malicious wrong when they disagree over what objects are the rightful property they have recognized, to defraud one another by using the contractual form of reciprocal recognition to acquire property through misrepresentation, and to commit crimes by simply choosing to violate openly the property rights of others. As Hegel argues, the interaction of persons provides no higher authority to adjudicate conflicts of entitlement or to punish fraud and crime with an objectively recognized use of force. All it offers are persons on an equal footing. Consequently, any attempt by a person to right a wrong is always subject to being a further wrong, for so long as the parties involved choose not to recognize the attempt as rightful retribution, it remains an illegitimate act of revenge.[5]

This means that the reality of abstract right not only has certain historical preconditions, but also requires the coexistence of additional structures of justice to resolve the internal dilemmas of property relations. In Hegel's view, abstract right does not thereby become the *principle* of derivative relations of justice, reinstating the aporias of liberty. Rather, abstract right becomes the most rudimentary component of a more encompassing reality of freedom, whose other forms of right all presuppose and refer to personhood as an *element* of their own specific interaction.

Logically enough, Hegel concludes that, in the first instance, the deficient abstractness of personhood calls into play a mode of self-determination in which individuals recognize that only through their own action towards others will right be brought into existence, and that only in realizing it will their own conduct have normative validity. On this basis individuals interact not simply as persons, giving their wills a particular embodiment in property, but as moral subjects who make it their own intention to do right in general, and to that extent recognize one another as rightfully responsible for their own actions.

In effect, Hegel's positive sublation of Kantian practical reason here reaches the point of incorporating its moral standpoint into the interaction of freedom. However, as Ritter makes clear in "Morality and Ethical Life," this incorporation involves a fundamental recasting of Kantian morality.

Although Hegel here grants moral subjectivity its valid right, he does not conceive it as an inner determination of the self. Instead, he develops it as an intersubjective structure consisting in action towards others which is recognizably related to the inner intention of its author. Hegel holds that an individual can actually determine himself morally only by taking action that affects other subjects and is prefigured in a conscious purpose positively relating to their right and welfare. Such action is indeed of interest for the right and welfare of the doer himself, but only within the context of the plurality of moral subjects. That plural context affords the sphere for the realization of what is morally right, and thus the constitutive framework for moral action itself. Accordingly, throughout Hegel's discussion of purpose and responsibility, intention and welfare, and good and conscience, moral subjects always stand in relation to one another through actions they have respectively intended. Without acting towards others they have not determined themselves morally, whereas without intending what they do, their behavior has no morally accountable character.

As Ritter notes, Hegel here pays due regard to the role of inner intention in morality, which Kant so emphasizes, without neglecting the equally critical side of action that Kant ignores. Hegel's negative critique of practical reason already indicated that both sides must be present if there is to be any moral willing at all. In his reformulation of the moral standpoint, Hegel now provides the positive lesson: moral actions are only those deeds which are prefigured in conscious purpose, whereas the moral intention of purpose concerns only those consequences of a real action which are relevant to the realization of right and welfare.[6]

Significant though these internal transformations are, what most radically marks Hegel's departure from the Kantian moral standpoint is the status morality is given as a particular mode of interaction. Whereas Kant makes morality the one firm basis of normative validity, from which only legality can be distinguished as a derivative sphere, Hegel takes morality to be a form of self-determination which not only presupposes abstract right, but serves as a bridge to independent structures of ethical life that Kant cannot conceive.

As much as abstract right calls for moral action, the required relations of morality are, for Hegel, themselves inherently problematic. On the one hand, moral subjectivity has its own valid self-determination only insofar as it realizes the universal good encompassing right and welfare as the objective unconditioned end of action. On the other hand, this moral good lacks all particular determination within itself precisely because it is an unrealized ought which can only be brought into existence through the self-determination of the moral subject. Therefore, although the moral subject should have good intentions and bring into being what is objectively valid, the good in question is itself utterly abstract and can only be determined by the particular subjectivity of conscience. Conscience, however, cannot arrive at determinations that are objectively valid because all it has to rely on is its own subjective choice as to what is good. Consequently the structure conscience provides for determining the good is just as empty and abstract as the good itself.[7]

Although this implicit identity of the good and conscience seals the uncertainty and anguish in which morality must proceed, it provides the basis for the interaction of ethical life, to which Hegel moves in virtue of thinking through the structure of moral action. As Ritter stresses, this transition from morality to ethical life relegates moral subjectivity to a subordinate position within the total structure of justice, while no less preserving it as a valid, if troubled component. In this regard, Hegel's move entails a clear break with both Kantian and classical Greek theories of justice. Whereas Kant collapsed all right into morality and legality, Plato and Aristotle excluded the subjective reflection of moral conscience from their concept of ethical institutions. By contrast, Hegel here introduces an ethical life irreducible to abstract right and morality, which nevertheless incorporates their respective freedoms in its ethical order.

What makes this especially significant for the evaluation of modernity is that Hegel's ensuing development of ethical life brings to a head the *de jure* question of what justice is, by providing the structures of interaction affording freedom its totality. Indeed, the determinations of abstract right and morality already make certain judgments possible. In "Person and Property" Ritter has documented how Hegel considers the correlative desacralization of nature and universalization of personhood to be works in progress of the modern era. In "Morality and Ethical Life" Ritter goes on to show that Hegel recognizes moral subjectivity to have begun to win its due as a valid mode of freedom only in modernity. On both counts, modern relations would seem to exhibit intrinsically just forms of self-determination.

Nevertheless, if the reality of freedom is crowned by ethical life, the presence of abstract right and morality can hardly sanctify modern times by themselves. The encompassing institutions of ethical life would have to be present as well, for only then would modernity be a world of justice, in which the philosophy of right could be the age grasped in thought, because the Idea of freedom was actually at hand.

The Unprecedented Ethical Life of Civil Society and the State

At first glance, what Hegel develops as ethical life are institutions familiar enough in modern times: namely, the family, society, and the state. What is not so usual is that these three spheres are conceived to be structures of interaction which are ethical in character.

As interaction structures, they are, like personhood and morality, normatively valid relations between individuals, consisting in specific modes of reciprocal self-determination.

What distinguishes them as spheres of ethical life is that they are institutions of freedom in which the particular self-determination of their members has its realization in the common structures of the ethical community to which they belong and through which they act. As Ritter notes, whereas Kant left autonomy without reality by restricting ethics to the inner legislation of moral duty while relegating all external relations (including property, family, civil government, and world law) to the non-ethical sphere of legality, Hegel here conceives the family, civil society, and the state as ethical interactions precisely insofar as they give subjective freedom actuality by being the existing framework of its realization. In contrast to morality, where the universal good is an ought to be, ever opposed to the particular willing of conscience, ethical life comprises an interpenetration of universal and particular, where the individual has free reality because the family, society, and state in which he acts have the realization of his freedom as their substance.

Hegel recognizes that it is no more self-evident how the special unity of ethical life works itself out than how the family, society, and the state can provide the modes of its existence. Accordingly, in the *Philosophy of Right*, he attempts to show that the minimal determination of ethical life comprises the unity of the family, that this unity entails the further ethical order of civil society into which the family is incorporated, and finally, that civil society both requires and provides the prerequisites for the state, whose political bonds of recognition bring ethical life to an encompassing whole.

In terms of this sequence, what is of preeminent importance is the relationship of civil society and the state, for on it depends the total structure of ethical life. Appropriately, Ritter focuses attention on this relation in examining Hegel's ethical judgment of modernity.

To a certain extent, the whole relation is a novel one, for although Hegel is not the first to coin the term "civil society," he is generally recognized to be the first to conceive civil society in radical distinction from the state. Previously politics was conceived either in the classical Greek fashion, as the exclusive domain of public life in contrast to the household, or, in the manner of the liberal tradition, as a *civil* government, whose duties were a function of a civil society that itself derived from a naturally determined liberty. By comparison, Hegel demarcates civil society from the state by having the economy, social interest groups, and the public administrations of civil law and welfare all fall within civil society as necessary components of social freedom, while making the independent concern of self-government the specific activity and raison d'être of the state. On this basis, Hegel gives an entirely new mandate to public life.

To begin with, by conceiving civil society as a separate sphere of ethical life, he bestows normative validity upon a community

of interest whose institutions allow individuals to relate to one
another solely by pursuing particular ends of their own choosing which can be realized only in conjunction with the similar
pursuits of others.

As Ritter points out, this basic interaction structure of civil
society detaches its members from all traditional custom and hierarchy and sets them on the equal footing of their caprice and
desire, free to exercise the right of acting in public for their own
interest to the degree that the interests of others are thereby
advanced. In this regard, civil society becomes a power of division and dichotomy, separating individuals from the given
bonds of the historical past, and setting them against one another as bearers of particular ends, whose only positive relation
is that of mutual dependence.

Nevertheless, Hegel recognizes this very disunion to be an *ethical* unity, because it not only liberates individuals from externally imposed ties but also establishes the series of institutions
in which the freedom of particularity achieves a normatively
valid realization. Civil society is therefore indispensible, for
without its social right, public life becomes a constraint upon its
members, neither embodying their chosen interests, nor allowing them the free reign to relate to others for particular ends of
their own.

Significantly, Hegel conceives economic relations to be the basic institutional structure of civil society. Most interpreters other
than Ritter have taken this to mean that Hegel follows the path
of the classical political economy of Steuart, Smith, and Ricardo,
since they also developed the economy within what they too
called civil society. What these interpreters ignore is that the
"civil society" of the political economists is distinguished not
from an independent political sphere, but from a "civil government" devoted to the same civil rights, deriving from liberty,
which are supposedly operative in the market place. Accord-

ingly, its economy can be called a "political" economy insofar as the ends ascribed to politics are ultimately indistinguishable from those of society.

Nothing could be further from Hegel's approach. Because he radically demarcates civil society from the state and conceives both as structures of interaction independent of natural determination, what he develops is not a political, but a thoroughly *social* economy. In so doing, Hegel initiates a critique of political economy which not only outstrips that of Marx and his followers, but makes them its victim.[8]

They, of course, have striven to eliminate the natural reductions of political economy, and determine all economic relations as social in character. In working out their theory, however, Marxists have generally continued to conceive need, utility, and use-value production as natural givens of the human condition.[9] Furthermore, they have judged the state to be an instrument of class interest, better done away with, thereby advancing a position which takes the liberal conflation of civil society and state to its logical extreme.

Hegel, on the contrary, first shows that economic need, utility, and use-value production owe their character to social interaction. As Ritter points out, although civil society does relate its members to one another through their need make-up, it does not do so as a natural condition. It rather builds an historically emergent framework in which individuals act to satisfy not their physical requirements or psychological desires, but those freely chosen needs whose means of satisfaction can only be had through other analogously needy individuals. Although the particular content of these *economic* needs remains a matter of personal preference, it is no less predicated upon the relations between the individuals bearing them. If these relations are such that individuals can satisfy their biological needs without entering into interaction with one another, then these needs have no economic character and reality. Thus, the need make-up at play in economic interaction is socially determined from the outset, and does not involve needs whose objects either lie already in the private domain of the individual or are freely available from nature.

Hegel accordingly points out that economic need is not satisfied with mere natural or psychological things, such as the air we must breathe or the affections we desire, but with *commodities*, goods expressly owned by other members of civil society who are willing to exchange them to satisfy their own social wants. As he further points out, in opposition to political economists and Marxists alike, these commodities possess utility which is social and not natural in character, for they satisfy the specifically social needs of interested individuals encountering their owners, rather than the wants of human nature. Consequently, the production of goods possessing utility is equally a social matter, predicated upon civil society's system of interdependent needs. As Hegel notes, a product can have economic use-value only by being fashioned as a commodity for the needs of other individuals.[10] By contrast, all natural, subsistence production has no economic reality on its own, for the wants, work, and products it involves relate man and nature, instead of relating individuals to one another in the civil interaction of the economy.

What all this entails is that economic relations proceed through acts of commodity exchange, where individuals acquire what they need from someone else by voluntarily giving in return some good of their own which that other individual correlatively seeks to have. In this way, the basic relations between the members of civil society are mediated by commodities.

Needless to say, the justice of this mediation has been called into question, most notably by Marx, who argues that commodity exchange gives rise to the reification of commodity fetishism, where the social relations between individuals figure as relations between things ruling over men's lives. Ritter points out, however, that Hegel's conception of economic interaction suggests how the exact opposite is the case.

First of all, in commodity exchange, the goods through which individuals interact are not things but social objects of the will bearing value in virtue of the interdependent self-determinations of their owners. Secondly, commodity exchange takes place only insofar as the participating individuals recognize one another both as free persons, objectively owning their respective goods, and as free members of civil society, exercising the common right of satisfying needs of their own choosing. Instead of encountering one another as subjects of things, they lord over their commodities, using them as means to interact as independent bearers of need, enjoying the recognized freedom to pursue their particular ends in public. Accordingly, engaging in commodity exchange is an ethical right, for it realizes the particular self-determination of the individual in unity with the existing system of the economy.

Hegel recognizes, however, that civil society can neither restrict itself to economic relations nor permit them to have free sway. The rudimentary reason for this is that the economy cannot guarantee the realization of the very needs its interaction generates. Precisely because the economy consists in commodity relations resting on mutual agreements of exchange, it is a matter of contingency whether its members encounter other willing parties whose respective needs and goods correlate with their own. Hegel draws the unavoidable conclusion: so long as the economy is left to its own logic of interdependent self-determinations, there is nothing to prevent economic relations from resulting in crises, overproduction, unemployment, and an amassing of riches by some and a growing poverty of others.

As Ritter indicates, this is a matter of injustice due to civil society's own ethical relations. Unemployment and poverty may not be violations of abstract right, but they are social wrongs once economic interaction has established the civil right of individuals to pursue and satisfy their chosen needs for commodities.

The important point is that although Hegel is certainly struck by the glaring disparities of wealth in the economies of his day, he does not view this as an historical disease afflicting a certain stage of economic development. Rather, he considers it a problem endemic to economic relations, which reveals their limited justice.

Hegel holds, as a result, that civil society cannot reduce itself to an economy. On the one hand, it must allow its members to organize into social interest groups to press for what the economy does not deliver on its own. On the other hand, it must also contain an administration of civil law and a public administration of welfare to guarantee and enforce the personhood of its members and their right to satisfy their needs through their own free action. Since all these public institutions operate on the basis of the economy, they do not annul or replace commodity relations, but rather regulate them so that the ethical right of economic action has its intrinsic contingency externally resolved. Although the economy thereby remains the basic structure of civil society to which public administration refers, its own justice mandates that it be a subordinate and not a determining base of society.

In arriving at this differentiation of social institutions, Hegel's development of civil society thus effectively demonstrates how the economy must have a subordinate position within society if social freedom is to be realized.

There is, however, another, even more decisive side to Hegel's subordination of economic relations that Ritter brings to light. It consists in the fact that the public administrations of civil law and welfare, which rule over the economy, are themselves *social* institutions falling within the community of interest of civil society. In contrast to liberals and Marxists alike, Hegel does not identify these institutions with the state, but explicitly characterizes them as civil, as opposed to political, institutions. As Ritter points out, Hegel recognizes that the public enforcement of civil law and welfare is relative to the pursuit of particular ends constitutive of civil society. What these institutions realize are not political rights to participate in self-government, but the civil rights to enjoy one's person and property under the protection of public law and authority, and to have the publically guaranteed opportunity to satisfy one's own needs through action of one's own choosing. The activities of these institutions are thus not for their own sake, but for advancing the particular interests of the members of society. Even when this be so broadly defined as the public welfare, it is still an end which is separate from the administration of society. In other words, the institutions of civil law and public welfare neither provide the members of society with political freedom, nor comprise a self-determining government whose ruling activity is an end in itself and thereby politically sovereign.

Hegel draws the dual consequences of this limitation:

On the one hand, the public administration of civil society cannot be the crowning order of ethical life, for it leaves the structures of interaction without an institution of freedom which holds them all together in a self-determined whole.

On the other hand, any "liberalism" or "socialism" which reduces government to an administration of civil law and/or public welfare, undermines political freedom and must be rejected. As Ritter notes, Hegel explicitly attacks the "welfare state" in this regard for making government an instrument of civil society with no political ends of its own.

Accordingly, what civil society calls for is not civil government, a welfare state, or any political order based on class or other social interests. Rather, Hegel concludes in an unprecedented move, civil society demands a free political domain radically distinct from itself. The very limits of social freedom make necessary a sovereign state whose body politic gives freedom totality by integrating all interaction into its realm and determining that realm through its own self-governing activity as a self-determining whole.

Ritter himself does not discuss at length how Hegel actually develops the specific structures of the state. Indeed, Hegel's treatment of political institutions has received no sustained critique since Marx' early attempt,[11] which itself survives only in a very fragmented form. What Ritter does touch upon, however, is the basic character of the state as an ethical institution that incorporates all other relations of right within itself. This sets the highest general bounds of the interaction of freedom, and thus provides the ultimate measure for Hegel's judgment of modernity.

As Ritter indicates, Hegel's move beyond civil society gives politics a two-fold mandate.

On the one hand, the state must be an ethical association whose members interact not as civilians pursuing separate particular interests, but as citizens willing government policy as the end of their own free action, insofar as the state in which they act is itself the existing structure of their political freedom to govern themselves. In this ethical unity of universal and particular, individuals exercise their respected rights as citizens by willing the universal determination of the state, while the state has its sovereign validity for them by being the actuality of their particular political autonomy. Contrary to the "politics" of civil government, class rule, or the welfare state, the self-determination of the citizen is here participation in self-government because the body politic in which the individual can exercise that right has as its end, not particular interests or public welfare, but the realization of self-rule.

On the other hand, for the state to be this sovereign sphere of self-government, it cannot cancel the social freedom of interest or any of the other modes of recognized self-determination. This would set it against its own members and thereby destroy its constitutive ethical unity. Instead, the state must contain all these freedoms within itself, preserving their rights through its own rule, while maintaining its own sovereignty by preventing any of these component spheres from subordinating politics to their specific concerns.

The state must thus insure that its citizens enjoy their freedoms of personhood, moral subjectivity, family life, and social action, without allowing these to undermine their political freedom. In this regard, the state has the right to counter the arbitrariness of conscience when its acts violate the laws of the state, and even demand the lives of its members when needed to defend the political freedom of national sovereignty.

With respect to society, Hegel concludes, the state has a similarly dual relation. On the one hand, it must provide the administrations of civil law and public welfare with adequate legislated means to carry out their *social* regulation of the economy. On the other hand, the state must intervene in society on purely political grounds to insure that class struggles, economic power, and other social factors do not take hold of politics, preventing citizens from exercising self-rule and subordinating government policy to some social interest. Only by keeping civil society in its subordinate position can the state preserve its own freedom.

In this dual capacity, politics gives freedom totality by establishing the integral reality of all other modes of interaction through its own self-governing activity. As citizens of the just state, individuals thus attain for their part the freedom to determine the totality of practical life through their own willing.

Given this achievement of the state, the only remaining matter of right, besides the relations between states, is the question of the historical process whereby such a totality of freedom can come into existence. Hegel concludes his philosophy of right with this problem; and it is here that he finally judges modernity by asking whether the modern age is the historical epoch in which all the structures of interaction have finally come to the light of day.

Hegel's Judgment of Modernity

Ritter has established the importance of this judgment as it must be done, by laying out the basic outline of personhood, morality, and the ethical life of society and state in Hegel's conception of freedom. Having gone this far, he can proceed to introduce the judgment itself by indicating what the historical developments are that Hegel considers constitutive of modernity.

In the essays, "Hegel and The Reformation" and "Hegel and The French Revolution," Ritter shows how Hegel regards the modern age as determined by three unprecedented developments: the Reformation, the rise of capitalism in England, and the French Revolution.

Hegel understands the first of these, the Reformation, as having effected a liberation of religious conscience from external authority, which grants subjectivity the right to rely upon its own certainty in determining what holds valid for it. Accordingly, the Reformation has a just ethical dimension, for it carries with it the standpoint of morality, giving its independent conscience a respected existence. Hegel recognizes that this moral aspect of the Reformation has an intrinsic validity, and that its worldly presence does not preclude any other structures of interaction.

Nevertheless, the Reformation does not itself establish a secular order in which subjective freedom has its existing realization, even if it frees conscience from the rule of the church. Consequently, Hegel concludes, modernity must involve more than a Reformation if it is to bring justice into being.

As Ritter indicates, Hegel considers the rise of capitalism in England to provide a certain measure of the required complement to the Reformation—but not only that.

On the one hand, the economic development beginning in England has stamped the modern age with the most basic features of civil society. Capitalism has emancipated men from the hierarchy and natural determination of past tradition, desacralizing nature by subsuming it under the universal sway of commodity relations, and setting individuals against one another in the social equality of their interdependent need. It has put in motion the commodity circulation in which individuals can exercise their civil right to decide what they want and satisfy their needs through freely chosen action. In these respects, Hegel maintains, the capitalist development of modernity has established certain just relations of civil society.

However, as Ritter points out, Hegel also notes that the rise of capitalism has left necessary structures of civil society unrealized, and thereby distorted those relations which it has brought into being. Capitalism has certainly set loose the free activity of economic interaction, but it has not engendered the adequate social administration of the economy which must secure the public welfare. In England Hegel sees before him the full spectacle of the contingency of satisfaction endemic to economic relations—unprecedented wealth and poverty side by side, unemployment and overproduction, growing class antagonisms, and everywhere the spread of these troubled market relations beyond all given limit. Hegel does indeed witness attempts to remove the social injustice, but these either fail to curtail the unrelieved want or substitute a public dole for the guaranteed opportunity to satisfy one's needs through activity of one's own choosing.

In effect, capitalism represents for Hegel a society which is not fully civil because the economy is its determining base rather than a subordinate sphere ruled over by the civil administrations of justice and welfare. Modernity may have here introduced the basic economic structure of civil society, but it has not thereby realized social freedom in full. It has left that as unfinished business, which, Hegel notes, already confronts England with the threat of an uprising to transform its society.

The problem with capitalism, however, cannot be merely social in character. Given the dual relation of the state to civil society, the distorted character of modern society would have to be reflected in a corresponding failure of its political institutions. In turning finally to the French Revolution, as modernity's third determining development, Hegel finds the expected problem.

As Ritter points out, Hegel's political diagnosis has two sides.

On the one hand, Hegel grants, the French Revolution introduced the valid ethical notion that freedom is the legitimate substance of politics and that all members of the state have the right to be citizens and participate in self-government. Through the Revolution's own act, modernity has brought history to the point of sweeping aside all given authority and tradition and replacing them with institutions of freedom determined through the sovereign rule of a free state.

On the other hand, Hegel observes, the Revolution failed to carry out the actual constitution of freedom which it made the order of the day. Instead of erecting political institutions with ethical life's concrete unity of universal and particular, it offered the spectacle of ruling factions devouring one another in the name of the will of the people. Unlike the public autonomy of citizens in a duly constituted state, the people's will is something pre-political in origin, and its alleged unitary character excludes the plurality of interaction that can alone bring freedom, rather than arbitrary domination, into politics. By failing to establish organs of self-government, the Revolution put state power in the hands of particular usurpers whose claims of universality could not mask their inability to raise the body politic above the play of interests.

As for the concurrent attempts at restoration, Hegel recognized that they could offer no way out of the dilemma, either. Because they only reestablished traditional authority, the state remained without the legitimate sovereignty which political institutions of freedom could alone provide.

As a result, politics in modernity stands unable to assert its proper hegemony over social interest, and so realize the just relation between state and civil society.

Hegel realizes that this political failure does not just mean that society is left at bay before the free play of its economy. Rather, as Ritter points out, Hegel here sees modernity facing the critical danger of society overwhelming politics and all other spheres of interaction, making its own distorted relations the real determining base of practical life.

Consequently, Hegel must finally conclude that modernity cannot be granted legitimacy. Although it has introduced fundamental elements of personhood, morality, civil society, and the state, it has not brought into being the totality of ethical life. Therefore, modernity stands as a yet open chapter in the unfinished history of freedom's emergence.

Hegel has no predictions to offer, but only the observation that in the years to come the fate of justice will hinge upon the unresolved problems of civil society and the state.

A century and a half has passed since Hegel delivered his judgment on modernity. Other revolutions and restorations have come and gone, and their protagonists have defined themselves as much in reference to Hegel as to anything else. Nevertheless, whether our own day has confronted the lessons of the philosophy of right and advanced toward the realization of social and political freedom remains a very real question.

In contemporary liberal democracies, the economic domination of society and the social subordination of politics that Hegel feared has often been acknowledged. Most criticism has fallen on the condition of public welfare as it lies under the relatively free sway of commodity relations; but the condition of politics is no less suspect when judged against Hegel's concept of the state. The ethical unity of politics is lacking when citizens exercise only their civil rights, while leaving actual governing to parties who monopolize political activity as a private vocation of professional politicians. Where citizens are appealed to not as participants in self-government, but as private members of society, taxpayers rather than citizens, bearers of class, ethnic, or other particular interests rather than as subjects of political interaction, they can only answer back either by taking infrequent and ill-attended trips to the ballot box (which reestablish the same gulf between citizen and government), by taking to the streets (which involves no wielding of political power but only an attempt to influence those who govern), or by responding with the voice of public opinion (wherein a passive, atomized mass of individuals express their personal preference instead of engaging in governing themselves).

Although today's social democratic regimes may realize the public administration of welfare more thoroughly than the liberal state, their professed subordination of government to that end results in the characteristic distortion of the welfare state, which Hegel attacked for reducing politics to a civil management of the public welfare.

Viewed from the standpoint of the *Philosophy of Right*, contemporary communist regimes bring this social reduction to a greater extreme, while striking at civil freedom as well. A one-party worker state explicitly subordinates political power to a particular class interest and also restricts the interaction of social groups such that the working class is itself unable to express and advance the interest on which the state is supposedly founded. As a result, the interaction of politics is supplanted by the single will of a party, whose domination of society leaves its own interest the sole arbiter of public affairs.

Finally, Hegel's conception of right has its total opposite in Nazi rule, which accomplishes a complete destruction of political and social interaction, in which the natural determination of a people replaces freedom as the basis of state and society, with political power concentrated in the natural will of a leader who stands above all reciprocal relations as the immediate expression of a master race.

If these are the regimes which modernity has left at our door, the challenge of Hegel's philosophy of right has only grown stronger with the passage of time. This challenge is at once theoretical and practical, and it is the ultimate achievement of Ritter's essays to have raised it with all the urgency it warrants today. In face of the open history of freedom, it is our affair whether the theory of interaction will remain ignored, or whether thinkers will pursue its arguments further while citizens choose to make them the basis of political action.

Notes

1. See par. 2 and the note to par. 3 in Hegel's *Philosophy of Right* (PR), translated by T. M. Knox, Oxford University Press, New York 1967.

2. See 1113a33–35, 1176a13–16, 1176b25, 1284a3–34, 1288a27–28, and 1288a32–b4 in Aristotle's *Nicomachean Ethics* (1094a–1181b) and *Politics* (1252–1324b).

3. M. B. Foster has discussed this point at length with reference to Hegel's critique of Plato's *Republic* in his neglected work, *The Political Philosophies of Plato and Hegel*, Oxford University Press, London 1968.

4. Hannah Arendt has emphasized this in her important critique of modern revolutions, which applies Hegel's distinction of society and state, without, however, recognizing the legitimacy of civil society's subordinate structure of freedom. See Hannah Arendt, *On Revolution*, Viking, New York 1976.

5. See PR pars. 82ff. and 102.

6. See PR 117 and 125.

7. See PR 141.

8. For examples of current attempts to pursue this critique further, see David P. Levine, *Economic Theory*, Routledge and Kegan Paul, London 1978, and Richard Dien Winfield, *The Social Determination of Production: The Critique of Hegel's System of Needs and Marx' Concept of Capital*, diss. Yale University 1977.

9. For a critique of these natural reductions see Winfield, *op. cit.*, pp. 164–188, and Richard Dien Winfield, "The Social Determination of the Labor Process from Hegel to Marx," *Philosophical Forum*, vol. 11, no. 3.

10. See PR 192 and 196.

11. See Karl Marx, *Critique of Hegel's "Philosophy of Right,"* Cambridge University Press, London 1970. In what remains of this text, Marx makes two important observations. He shows that Hegel's characterization of the head of state as a monarch involves a natural determination of royal birth that violates the proper freedom of political interaction. Secondly, Marx rightly points out that Hegel's insertion of Estates as institutional elements of the legislature (paragraphs 301ff.) makes class interest a determining factor in politics, contrary to the basic separation of civil society and state. Both of these inconsistent features must be removed if political interaction is to be properly conceived in its ethical universality. Marx, however, never made the necessary revisions, but instead finally accepted the originally liberal notion that politics can never rise above particular

interests. Accordingly he called for the withering away of the state and the building of a communist society, where public freedom is eliminated in favor of a technical domination of nature that sets men "free" to engage in the purely private activities of their natural species being.

Hegel and the French
Revolution (1956)

I

1. The critical consideration of Hegel's political philosophy following the appearance of the *Philosophy of Right* (1821)[1] was brought to a close by Rudolf Haym's *Lectures On Hegel and His Time*.[2] Hegel, branded "the philosophical dictator of Germany" (Haym p. 357), was found guilty of having made philosophy "the scientific dwelling of the spirit of Prussian restoration" (359), providing "the absolute formula" to "political conservatism, quietism and optimism" (365), and thereby of placing himself in the service of the "scientifically formulated justification of the Karlsbad police system and the persecution of demagogues" (364).[3]

Proof of this is found in the fact that Hegel did after all accept the appointment at Berlin,[4] and in his critique of Fries as "a ringleader of these hosts of superficiality, of these self-styled 'philosophers'" (PR p. 5), a critique amounting to a political denunciation, touching in the first place Hegel's own philosophy itself. It placed the theory of state and society under the tenet that the rational is real and the real is rational, and therewith, according to Haym, politically took on the task of justifying reality "as it stood in Prussia in 1821" (Haym p. 366). It had further linked the state with the predicates of the divine, the absolute, reason, and ethical substance in order to deify its power and set it against the freedom of the individual. For Haym, the reactionary intention and function of Hegel's philosophy is proven by the deification of the state and by the justification of reality as rational.

His lectures therefore take up the task of banning Hegel's system from the present and "returning it to the expired or half-expired life in which it had its basis," in order so to set it aside like a "tombstone" in the "great edifice of eternal history" (8).

Haym's critique was effective. For decades Hegel's philosophy remained without influence; the repute of statism and of the reactionary absolutization of state power has persisted till today. One still cannot speak of Hegel's political philosophy without having to reckon with the image of the Prussian reactionary Hegel.[5]

The statements on which Haym grounds his charge of state deification are located above all in the *Philosophy of Right*. Hegel here calls the state the "actuality of the ethical Idea" (par. 257) and what is "absolutely rational" (par. 258). It is spirit "which gives itself its actuality in the process of *World-History*" (par. 259) and is the "power of reason actualizing itself" in "the march of God in the world" (par. 258 Addition). Because the state is the world "which mind has made for itself," one should "venerate the state as a secular deity" (par. 272 Addition).

All these assertions are for Hegel himself metaphysical assertions; he methodically relates the *Philosophy of Right* to the *Logic*;[6] it differentiates itself from an "ordinary compendium" through its "logical spirit" and its "speculative way of knowing" (PR 1, 2). Metaphysics is here understood by Hegel in the sense of its traditional determination as the theoretical science of the being of what is; it has to conceive "what is" (11) as the presence of the "substance which is immanent and the eternal which is present" (10). The statements taken exception to by Haym thus signify that Hegel incorporates state and society into metaphysical theory and understands them as the realization (*actualitas*) of being in historical existence, whereby being remains identical for him with reason and the divine of the philosophical tradition. In the same sense Aristotle and St. Thomas called the "philosophical life" and its theory "divine" in order to differentiate it from practical knowledge. Philosophy grounds its arguments in the divine and not in the necessity of practical life; it is therefore itself godly, because it gathers itself around the divine (*divina quia de divinis*).[7] In the context of this tradition—Hegel presupposes it and always did understand his philosophy as a realization of the one, eternally self-same philosophy[8]—the statements of the *Philosophy of Right* that are politically objectionable to Haym mean for Hegel himself that the state has for its content man in his relation to the divine and not only in his needful nature, as is the case in natural theories of society. Therefore its task is one of making possible the innerworldly realization of the spiritual, religious, and ethical orders borne by human existence.

The same metaphysical meaning is found in the other proposition Haym condemned as reactionary, that of the identity of reality with reason: "What is rational is actual and what is actual is rational" (10). It expresses the root thought of all philosophy, that the unity of being and reason is the grounding substance of reality and its truth. For Hegel, it thus recalls in the present the idea in terms of which philosophy always conceived itself, ever since Parmenides taught the identity of thought and being and Anaxagoras elevated reason to the principle of the world.[9] With this, however, Haym's critique of Hegel becomes philosophically important. What brings him to see in these metaphysical statements a politically intended, reactionary justification of the given political relations is not the conviction that philosophy idealizes and demands too much of political reality; *what is objectionable for Haym lies rather in the fact that Hegel applies metaphysical theory to contemporary society and its state.* This contemporary society is modern civil society, based on technology and science; with it, according to Haym, a new principle and a new age has arisen, "in which, thanks to the great technological discoveries of the century, matter has come to appear to be alive" and "the most basic foundations of our physical as well as our spiritual life have been torn down and reordered" (Haym 5). As a result of this reordering, theology and metaphysics have become antiquated and have lost their truth: The "stars of belief have fallen to the earth" (9), speculative philosophy has "been set aside by the progress of the world and by living history" (6). What formerly counted as an "objective ideal" and as something "eternal and fixed" has been reduced "to something purely historical" and "pragmatically realized" (9). For Haym, the Hegelian concepts of being, the divine, and the absolute have therefore lost all positive content and all contemporary truth with the emergence of modern society. Accordingly, their present employment can only be understood as a work of "reaction" which has no other sense than that of calling into question the new society, freed from "Heaven." The "rehash" of implicitly refuted metaphysical theory becomes for Haym an ideological truth intended to transfigure the powers of backwardness and of opposition to progress in the glory of a godliness that has become meaningless in itself. Hegel's philosophy, as philosophy, has become in principle a thing of the past because the present age has freed itself from metaphysics and theology. Therefore it is worth contributing to its demise; it must necessarily "go bankrupt because this entire branch of business lies ill" (5); within the arena of civil society it has no contemporary significance left; it has become reactionary.

2. Many who gladly follow Haym in speaking of Hegel's deification of the state would identify themselves less gladly with the argument that, in Haym's view, proves this state deification. Nevertheless, what alone still gives Haym's critique of Hegel's metaphysics of the state a contemporary philosophical significance is that Haym proceeds from the emancipation of modern society and therewith grounds his critique. Speculative philosophy already lost all actuality for Jakob Burckhardt and Nietzsche; for them, it was but a constructing and opining, "a gothic skyward blustering."[10] In contrast, the critique of Hegel by Haym and the liberal left has the great positive significance of still being aware of the political actuality of Hegel's philosophy and presupposing it. Haym grasped that in Hegel's philosophy, Hegel brought to a head, no less profoundly and ardently than his opponents, the problem of the contemporary age and of the society that emerged politically with the revolution in France and just as sweepingly with the formation of industry in England, and that stood ready to become the reality of the day. *Thereby Hegel becomes an opponent pure and simple; he conceives the same society, which in Haym's view brings about the liberation from that heaven of theology and metaphysics, as comprising the presence and appearance of the rational substance which from time immemorial has been the truth of reality and history according to philosophy.*[11]

In effect, Hegel's political philosophy gets dealt with here in terms of its own proper problem and its own proper concern. The *Philosophy of Right* makes state and society, encompassed in the concept of right, the content of speculation; it is in accord with this that the preface first takes up the traditional definition of *cognitio speculativa entis qua entis* and proceeds from it as knowledge of (being-)reason: "To comprehend what is, this is the task of philosophy, because what is, is reason" (11). Now, however, something follows which is encountered in this form altogether for the first time in the history of philosophy. *Hegel equates traditional metaphysical theory directly as such with knowledge of the age and the present.* Philosophy *as* knowledge of being is *at the same time* "its own time apprehended in thoughts" (11).

The humanities attend to spiritual education, art, poetry, and science as an expression of their age, to be understood as an objectification and shape of historical life. The Hegelian idea of philosophy as something of "its own time" cannot, however, be understood in this general cultural historical sense; it would thereby be disarmed and neutralized; the decisive actuality would be taken from it; for Hegel does not reflect upon the historical character of philosophy and spirit in general—he wishes to determine the contemporary development of metaphysics. For him, it can remain knowledge of being when, and only when, it is at the same time knowledge of its own age.

What is this conflation of philosophy and the interpretation of the present supposed to mean? Metaphysically speaking, the present signifies in the first instance the presence of being (of substance); it is present in coming into being and passing away, and appears in its abiding presence in the here and now. Thus Aristotle calls the object of philosophy that which "is now and of old and always sought after" (Met. VII, 1), and Hegel himself uses the concept of the present first in order to indicate with it the speculative object as such; it is "reason as an actual world before our eyes" (PR 12), "the substance which is immanent and the eternal which is present" (10). For Hegel, presence metaphysically considered is above all the presence of that which always was, always is, and always will be.

Nevertheless, Hegel at the same time goes beyond this metaphysical concept in his identification of philosophical thought with the thought of the age; he raises the question of how the presence of being can be found in the present age, since it has now become questionable and problematic. With modernity, a new reality stepped into history, which—for the first time in the

Western tradition—fundamentally set "outside itself" philosophy and its truth; the present age has begun to look back upon them as bygone matters that are dead for it; it has "lying behind itself" "so many philosophical systems" that it only augments "the extant collection of mummies and the general heap of contingent oddities" (*The Difference Between Fichte's and Schelling's System of Philosophy*, pp. 85, 86). For Hegel this has occurred; the age which philosophy has to grasp in thought is its own epoch, because this epoch for itself no longer seems to have anything in common with the One Philosophy or with what it had preserved in previous history. The present has emancipated itself from the philosophical tradition; the question of the essence of the historical-political present and its truth becomes in this time and hour a question of metaphysics in which the continuity of its history and tradition has become broken and problematic. In the identification of philosophy with the theory of its age, Hegel thus takes up the problem of the emancipation from historical heritage. For him, however, the radicality of its problematization comes forth not only in historical and social emancipation as such. The magnitude of the danger connected with it first shows itself in the fact that the "subjectivity" which seeks to preserve the divine religiously and philosophically, by rescuing it from what has become a godless present and investing it in inner spirit and nature, actually gives up the truth of the divine with this very rescue; it sees the emancipation in its retreat from the present world, such that, for Hegel, the subjective preservation becomes a mere appearance of itself. As a romantic flight from actuality, it presupposes that the divine has lost its power over objective reality. Certainly it has always been possible to seek the presence of being immediately in nature, and to honor nature as its appearance without bothering about the historical-political present. From time immemorial philosophy has conceived reason also as the "eternal harmony" of nature and as "the law and essence immanent within it" (PR 4). However, when this occurs today, the unresolved problem of the age and its historical emancipation stands simultaneously behind it. Because state and society, comprising the ethical world, no longer "enjoy the good fortune" "that it is reason which has achieved power and mastery within that element and which maintains itself and has its home there" (4), one now seeks, as in retreat, to redeem present reason in nature, in order to be able still to find it somewhere, like the "philosopher's stone." In this manner, the divine gets limited to nature *because* political reality has stepped beyond its realm, *because* state and society have been "left to the mercy of chance and caprice, to be God-forsaken" and thus have the ever existing truth "outside" themselves (4). This readiness to acknowledge the disengagement from the historical tradition thus becomes for Hegel the sign which signals the danger of emancipation in its full magnitude. One begins to search for God in nature, one wishes to redeem in nature the divine which the historical-political present has excluded from itself. The political upheaval of the age has called into question the meaning of the metaphysical tradition and its truth; it sets out to annihilate it. In Hegel's view, however, that also means that philosophy is faced with the question of how it is to react to this. Does the old world of spirit and its historical tradition come to its demise in the present with the emergence of modern society? Has the time arrived to undo its religious, ethical, spiritual substance and dismiss it as something past and over with historically? Philosophy can no longer evade these questions; there is no redemption through flight to nature or inner spirit. A "simple family remedy" no longer helps where the "millenary labor of reason and its intellect" has become questionable (6). Evasion of the posed problem is already its abandonment. Therefore the only path that remains open is taking up the problem of emancipation in its full radicality; Hegel sets out on this course by summoning the aid of the One Philosophy and making its theory the theory of the age and of the upheaval coming to pass within it.

II

3. For Hegel, the French Revolution is that event around which all the determinations of philosophy in relation to its time are clustered, with philosophy marking out the problem through attacks on and defenses of the Revolution. Conversely, there is no other philosophy that is a philosophy of revolution to such a degree and so profoundly, in its innermost drive, as that of Hegel.

Hegel was born in 1770 and died in 1831. He could never have looked back upon the Revolution as a settled occurrence viewed from the shore of a secured world. All that fills the period from 1789 till 1830 is also—in hope and fear—his own destiny, in which it is necessary to stand and prevail: the upheaval in France itself, its surge across Europe and Germany, the wars of Napoleon (which were always wars of revolution in Hegel's view), his collapse, the attempts to counter the driving revolutionary forces with the restoration of the old world, the ferment of the period, in which nothing is decided and everything remains open, unresolved, unsettled, up till the new uprising of 1830 foreseen by Hegel. "I am," he writes to Creuzer on October 30, 1819, "exactly fifty years old, I have passed thirty of them in this eternally agitated time of fearing and hoping, and I hoped that for once this fearing and hoping would be done with. Now I am forced to see that it goes on without halt, indeed, in troubled hours one imagines that it grows worse and worse" (Br. 359).

From beginning to end, his philosophy lives in this hoping and fearing. Hegel's very last written work, the essay *On the*

English Reform Bill, closes with the suggestion that there are forces at play which could very well surge forward to "introduce not reform but revolution."[12] Where revolution enters into the world—so it is written three decades earlier—there the age is torn out of its "calm satisfaction with the present" and its "patient acquiescence" (HPW 243). Revolution is the "tottering" of "things" (244). In relation to it, philosophy, which is in itself "something solitary," must become observant "of the history of the day" (Br. 85 to Zellman, January 23, 1807).[13]

What does this mean? Why does revolution and the events which follow it demand philosophical theory, the weighty concepts of being, the absolute, the divine, and ethical substance? Why does coming to grips with it finally lead to the metaphysical theory of the state, which then brings Hegel into discredit as a reactionary, a defender of what has become backward and outworn? The answer to these questions makes it necessary first to determine the relation in which Hegel stands to revolution, in order then secondly to grasp the problem around whose resolution his philosophy of revolution ultimately and properly revolves.

Hegel's encounter with the Revolution and his enthusiasm for it in his Tubingen period (1788–1793) stand at the beginning of his spiritual path. Everything proceeded from this enthusiasm; it sowed the friendship with Hölderlin and Schelling. Like "all noble Germans," the friends turned their attention at that time to the "proscribed philosophical spectacle" (Rosenkranz 32). In his Bern period Hegel is still filled with the thought of "revolution in Germany"; philosophy ought also to serve it. An "index of the age," it should come to be the "testimony" making "the halo disappear from around the leaders of the oppressors and the gods of the earth." It is now time for philosophy to show the peoples their "worth" so that they do "not ask for their rights which have been dragged through the dirt, but take them back themselves—appropriate them" (Br. 11 to Schelling, April 16, 1795).[14]

This passion for immediate participation and continuation begins to recede from approximately 1795 on. The experience of the Terror belongs henceforth to the tableau of the revolution. The *Phenomenology* (1807) already deals with it under the title: "absolute Freedom and Terror."[15] It is the "*fury* of destruction" (PS 359) to which the "meanest of all deaths" belongs, a death "which has no inner significance or filling" nor any "more significance than cutting off a head of cabbage or swallowing a mouthful of water" (360). This is "its self-destroying reality" (363), "the sheer terror of the negative" (362). That remains valid from now on and returns ever again.

For Hegel, the immediate consequence of this negativity of revolution is that it has discovered and brought about no lasting political solutions. It has been revealed, so Hegel judges in the last year of his life (PH 452), that "no political organization" gets "firmly established" with it. The constitutions get altered again and again and supercede one another; still now, "after forty years of war and confusion indescribable" where "a weary heart might fain congratulate itself on seeing a termination and tranquillization of all these disturbances" (451), "another breach . . . took place, and the Government was overturned" (451). Just as the contemporaneous writing on the *Reform Bill* closes with a look at the possible continuance of the Revolution, so at the end of the *Philosophy of History* there stands left the unresolved status of all the political problems thrown up by the Revolution: "Thus agitation and unrest are perpetuated" (452). The problem of political stabilization remains the "nodus . . . with which history is now occupied, and whose solution it has to work out in the future" (452). It is one of the few places where Hegel speaks at all about the future. He does it here with regard to the unresolved problem of the society constituted by the Revolution and its political order.

Nevertheless, neither the experience of the Terror nor the critical insight into the Revolution's inability to come to any positive and stable political solutions were able to turn Hegel into its opponent. For him, the positive mastery of the political problems that arose with it in history remained the task before which the age was unconditionally set. Hegel always affirmatively accepted the French Revolution; there is nothing more unambiguous than this affirmation, and yet it gets overlooked because the problem that is brought to a head in coming to grips with it later disappears from the age's view, thereby the context in which it unfolds then also becomes meaningless and, so to speak, invisible.

In the same section of the *Phenomenology* that places the Revolution under the concept of terror, Hegel at the same time maintains its necessity and the historical justice that makes it irresistible: "The undivided Substance of absolute freedom ascends the throne of the world without any power being able to resist it" (PS 357). This necessity is its historical justice, which remains determining for Hegel. In the *History of Philosophy* (first delivered as lectures in 1805–1806 in Jena, then twice in Heidelberg and six times in Berlin, the last time in 1829–1830), the causes which touched off the Revolution are still depicted with a feeling of partisanship that was in no way outstripped by the excitement of his youth. Its necessity is the contradiction between the developed feeling of freedom and the ruling "old institutions." They have become substanceless in this contradiction; the revolt must rise against them. Therewith the Revolution, and the philosophy preparing the way for it, certainly act "destructively," but what they destroy is something already destroyed in itself, the horrible condition of society, misery, meanness, shamelessness, and injustice of unbelievable degree, rightlessness of individuals with respect to law and politics, conscience, and thought. Against this, the storm broke loose out of necessity and with the justice of reason, such that Hegel calls the men "heroic" who prepared and kindled it "with splendid genius, with warmth and fire, with spirit and courage" (LHP III, 390). In 1817, the preface of the *Encyclopedia* alludes to the "youthful zest of the new epoch" "which has risen in the realm of science as well as politics"; it is greeted with "ecstasy" as the "rosy dawn" (VI, 8). In the same emphatic tone, the *Philosophy of History* calls the Revolution a "glorious mental dawn" (447): "All thinking beings shared in the jubilation of this epoch. Emotions of a lofty character stirred men's minds at that time; a spiritual enthusiasm thrilled through the world" (447). Thus, the expressions of unmistaken adherence and approval recur unequivocally and insistently from the time of his youth up till his last years. Every year Hegel thought back upon the storming of the Bastille and festively honored its day, while the experience remained for him one which no less insistently held before his eyes "the perils and terrors" (HPW 250).

Thus in Hegel's relation to revolution there belongs the enthusiasm for what has entered history with revolution together with the knowledge of the unresolved nature of its problems and of the necessity of its "collapse" into tyranny. The Revolution has posed the problem which the epoch has to work out. In its unresolvedness it thrusts out the question why neither the Revolution itself nor the revolutionary and restorative attempts of the following decades could succeed in arriving at political stability.

4. *This problem, posed and at the same time left unsolved by the Revolution, is that of the political realization of freedom.* The Revolution raised it to the "intellectual principle of the state" and set it in the "droits de l'homme et du citoyen" as a "natural right." For this reason, the "old framework of injustice" was unable to offer any resistance against it; the unique and unheard of aspect of the Revolution lies in the principle of freedom as justice: "A constitution . . . was established in harmony with the conception of Right, and on this foundation all future legislation was to be based. Never since the sun had stood in the firmament and the planets revolved around him had it been perceived" (PH 447).

Just as the people had raised it as their banner, so Hegel takes up the idea of freedom and makes it the "basic element" and "sole matter" of his philosophy.[16] This also signifies, however, that Hegel in this way makes philosophy the theory of the age; it is given the task of conceiving the political freedom of the Revolution in its essence; the foundation upon which the Revolution "bases all" shall be philosophically determined.

(a) According to Hegel, freedom is philosophically speaking the condition of man in which he can realize his humanity and so be himself and lead a human life. Freedom is thereby differentiated from the condition of man in which man does not have the option to be himself, and in which he has his being not in himself but in an other being which is not his own (as the slave in his master). Therefore Hegel understands freedom to be man's "self-contained existence (Bei-sich-selbst-seyn)": "Self-contained existence . . . is freedom . . . , for if I am dependent, my being is referred to something else which I am not; . . . I am free, on the contrary, when my existence depends upon myself" (PH 17). Freedom, as being at one with oneself, thus also entails that man can be "at home" in the world, that it not be foreign, but his own (PR par. 4 Addition, p. 226). It gives him freedom, when it allows him to be that which he can be as himself.

(b) With these elementary determinations Hegel extracts the concept of freedom from all the connections which have overlaid and mantled it in the course of centuries, and reaches back to its classical definition, which Aristotle gave it in the *Metaphys-*

ics: "Free is the man who wills for himself and not for an other."[17] For Aristotle, freedom is accordingly man's faculty of selfhood, and Hegel takes up this concept. This then becomes important also for his theory of political freedom. With Aristotle, political freedom is in the first instance the form of justice constitutive of the Greek city-state, the polis, through which the participation of the citizen (πολίτης) in the political decisions of the state, in the administration, legislation and judiciary are ordered and secured. This form of justice, however, is not itself politically grounded; it rather has its basis in the very freedom of the being of man, because to him who is free, and thus a man, necessarily also falls participation in political life. Thus for Aristotle, with the polis a political order has emerged in history which presupposes man's faculty of selfhood and has as its subject his substantial freedom and therewith man as man. For him, therefore, freedom as a political form of justice also contains the purpose of the political order; it must make possible the freedom of selfhood for every individual; he ought to live in the city as himself and be able to achieve his human determination, εὐδαιμονία.[18]

(c) Hegel adopts both the foundation of political freedom as justice in the substantial freedom of selfhood, and the material determination of the political order entailed in the end of making possible the realization of man's being and his freedom, and he has them bear fruit for his coming to grips with the French Revolution's idea of freedom. If one breaks through the "formalism" of the political confrontations and struggles and investigates the "content" of the Revolution[19] in order to bring to substantial determination what is ultimately of concern in all questions of a constitution, of the forming of law and state, then the philosophical doctrine of freedom makes possible the answer: *The problem which has been raised through the Revolution by the demand for political freedom consists in finding the legal form of free-*

dom and, that is, in developing a legal order which accords with the freedom of selfhood and does it justice, and enables the individual to be himself and achieve his human determination.

For Hegel, philosophy thus becomes the key which unlocks the door to the *positive* meaning of the new era coming to pass with the Revolution, a meaning buried and called into question by the factual course of the Revolution and the general unrest of the period following from it. While the Revolution itself and its theory constitute themselves in emancipation from all pre-given historical orders, and thus also determine themselves in opposition to the philosophical tradition, their positivity becomes graspable for Hegel precisely because he conceives the substantial freedom of philosophy as the foundation upon which "all gets based."

In Hegel's view, the unity of freedom and man's being is also the principle of world history; this has the very precise meaning, that history only becomes world history when it comes to have as its subject man in the sense of his being a man. Where man does not exist as man, there also history, whatever else it may signify, does not belong to world history. Its subject is man as man and therewith humanity. Since, however, man's human being necessarily includes freedom, Hegel understands world history also as the history whose principle is freedom and whose course has freedom's development and unfolding for its content. Philosophy thus "concerns itself . . . with the glory of the Idea mirroring itself in the History of the World . . . that which interests it is the recognition of the process of development which the Idea has passed through in realizing itself—i.e., the Idea of Freedom" (PH 457).

As history of man and of freedom, world history therefore begins for Hegel with the Greek polis, since in it "the consciousness of Freedom first arose." However, at the same time it holds true that the Greeks (and the Romans as well) only knew that "*some* are free, not man as such"; they had slaves, and with that, their "splendid liberty" was only an "accidental, transient and limited growth." The "rigorous thraldom of our common nature—of the Human" (18) still belonged to it. Christianity first brought to awareness that man as man is free and that thus all are to count as free and that freedom is the "most proper nature" of man. Through Christianity, freedom therefore becomes unrestrictedly identified with the being of man, and the history of the European peoples actually becomes world history to the degree that with Christianity its particular history widens into the history of man and his freedom.

Ever since the concept of world history lost all substantial meaning and became a mere collection for all known cultures and histories of peoples, there has hardly been any area in Hegel's philosophy so misunderstood and dismissed as mere speculation as the theory of world history. For Hegel himself, however, it is bound up with the theory of his own time and of the Revolution in a very immediate and fundamental sense.[20] The world-historical dimension of European history is the freedom of being human; that signifies, however, that *the Revolution itself must positively qualify as an epoch of European world history and its freedom of being human* insofar as it makes freedom the foundation upon which all legality is based. Hegel therefore calls it "in its substantial import . . . World-Historical" (452) and speaks of it as a "world-historical turning point," as the "condition of the world," and as forming an "epoch of the world's history" (LHP III, 385). This has a precise meaning that is indeed in contradiction to the Revolution's emancipatory self-determination, which excludes all connection with the history of its provenance. Namely, the Revolution must historically qualify as the event by which the "severe and lengthened process" of world history to permeate the state of the world with the freedom of being human (PH 18) is not only continued but brought to a close in a political sense. Whereas at the beginning of world history the citizens of ancient civil society had slaves and the unfree politically and legally alongside themselves, in the French Revolution, for the first time, political freedom taken as justice, and therewith man's capacity of selfhood, were raised to the principle and aim of society and state. Through it man first becomes without restriction the subject of the political order, "in virtue of his manhood alone, not because he is a Jew, Catholic, Protestant, German, Italian, etc." (PR par. 209, p. 31).

5. Hegel then finds it necessary to come to grips with the Revolution's emancipatory self-determination in immediate relation to this its positive world-historical content. However, what follows in the first instance from the insight into its world-historical meaning is that there is politically no longer any possibility of turning back from the Revolution and what it has achieved. *Every present and future legal and political order must presuppose and proceed from the Revolution's universal principle of freedom.* Against this, all reservations concerning its formalism and abstractness lose their force. After the polis entered into history in the ancient world and therewith, human being as the principle of justice (*Recht*) (albeit in restriction to the citizen and in exclusion of the slave), all political and legal forms which did not correspond to it had to become inessential for political theory. Plato and Aristotle therefore grounded political philosophy upon the polis alone. Where justice has become the justice of man, there justice which is not justice of man can only be called "justice" in a homonymous sense. The same holds for the French Revolution. After it made freedom for all, as men, the principle of right (*Recht*), all institutions and positive laws which contradict it lose by the process of historical necessity, every legitimate claim to validity, and in Hegel's view, this is true objectively as well as historically. The freedom constitutive for European world history is raised to the principle of all political and legal order by the Revolution. It is no longer possible to retreat from this principle. Right—now in principle the right of man—has attained the universality of the species; this cannot be restricted without leading to a contradiction with the human being of man and thereby with the new-won universal principle of all law.

In the discussion of concrete political relations and events in his political essays (*On the Recent Domestic Affairs of Wurtemberg, especially on the Inadequacy of the Municipal Constitution* of 1798, *The German Constitution* of 1800/3, the critical discussion of the *Proceedings of the Estates Assembly in the Kingdom of Wurtemberg* in the years 1815 and 1816, published in 1817 in the *Heidelberger Jahrbüchern,* and finally the essay *On the English Reform Bill* of 1830), in his letters, and elsewhere, Hegel comes to grips again and again, and sometimes ardently, with the political restoration. The real danger with the transformation that has come about is, especially in Germany, the passivity "to do nothing but wait confidently and blindly for the collapse of the old building, which is everywhere decaying and has its foundations undermined, and to submit to being crushed by the falling beams" (HPW 244). While, however, this "colorless and tasteless mediocrity maintains itself in the public realm" (Br. 255 to Niethammer, November 23, 1815)—an expression of the "nullity and irreality of public life" (*Ständeschrift* VI, 356) and of the prevailing "political deadness" (HPW 252)[21]—the world spirit continues along its path unrecognized, having "given the age the command to advance" (Br. 271 to Niethammer, July 5, 1816, compare LHP III, 158). This entails that all old historical institutions sanctified by tradition and custom fall into flux. "We stand," so it is stated in a lecture on speculative philosophy held in Jena at the end of 1806 (Dok. 352), "in an important epoch, a ferment, where spirit has jolted, emerged from its former shape, and gained a new one." Where this happens, "the entire mass of former representations and concepts, the bond of the world," disintegrates, and "collapses like a vision" (*ibid.*). That is the experience of the age. The last twenty-five years have proven themselves to be the "frightful pestle" in which "false concepts of law and prejudice about political constitutions" are crushed (HPW 282). Where a "new emergence of spirit" (Dok. 352) thus prepares itself, it is accordingly the task of philosophy "to greet and know" its new appearance "while others, resisting it powerlessly, cling to the past" (*ibid.*, compare PH 203f.).

In this manner Hegel stands in fundamental and immediate agreement with his conviction that in the Revolution the abiding world-historical substance brings itself to an actual present political realization, against which all attempts at restoration are a "powerless resisting."[22] They are in the wrong in principle, because and insofar as they pursue the reestablishment of institutions and positive laws that conflict with the principle of justice as the freedom of all, which the revolution has posited. For historical right then also loses its validity when "the justice and power, the wisdom and courage of times past; the honour and blood, the well-being and distress of generations long dead; and the relationships and manner which have perished with them . . . are expressed in the forms" of a constitution that stands in contradiction to "the life it . . . has now" (HPW 146) living within it. Therefore for Hegel, historical age is no principle that can found law or justify its preservation: "*An actual positive right a hundred years old rightly perishes if the basis conditioning its existence disappears*" (283). If, however, such positive law is nevertheless held on to or reestablished, then there arises a contradiction between "formality and reality"; and that leads necessarily to the political "non-existence" of reality (180). The unresolved problems of the present are made to disappear in the ostensible perseverance of the old forms *in the semblance of historical continuity*, while the "thing itself" is "no longer" and can "not possibly be brought back" (250)—when in reality, they drive on anarchically; the "vitality of the present day" is prevented from grasping itself in law (146). Hegel therefore calls such retention and reestablishment a "betrayal" (250). Against this, philosophy has to communicate the insights which can make possible a decision about it concerning what is tenable and what is untenable; the proper differentiation between what has rightfully passed away and what can be preserved must hold true as the sole justification and power "which can completely, honorably, and peaceably remove the tottering edifice and produce something safe in its place" (244).

What this differentiation of the tenable from what has become untenable, first formulated in the *Municipal Constitution* essay (1798), further signifies for Hegel's consideration of the restoration, manifests itself with particular insistence in the *Estates Assembly* essay of 1817.[23] In Wurtemberg the Estates had refused the offer of a constitution by the King; Hegel considers this refusal in this essay and takes the side of the King against the Estates; even so close a friend as Niethammer saw therein a reactionary position on the part of Hegel that was difficult to comprehend.[24] However, the true state of affairs is something else. The Assembly of the Estates could have thoroughly criticized or refused the constitution offered by the King with the argument that "it was contrary to the rights that subjects could claim in a political constitution on the strength of the eternal rights of reason" (274). They could then have placed themselves on the ground of the "modern" principle and discussed with the King the question of its political and constitutional realization. That, however, did not happen. The Estates rather rejected the royal constitution "on the ground that it was not the old constitution of Wurtemberg" and so was "not simply the restoration and revivification of the old constitution" (274). Herein lies the "fundamental error" of the Estates (281); it showed that they argued as "advocates of the old law"; therefore, not they, but the King represented the modern principle; therein lies the "perverse spectacle" (282) that these negotiations in Wurtemberg offered for Hegel. While the King brought "his constitution within the ambit of rational constitutional law" (282) and thus proceeded from the modern principle, "the Estates set themselves up as defenders of privileges and positive law" (282). This position of the Wurtemberg Estate representatives is exemplary for *what the restoration politically signifies and is in Hegel's view: the "extreme" of "rigid adherance to the positive constitutional law of a bygone situation" (282) and therewith precisely "the opposite of what started twenty-five years ago in a neighboring realm and what at the time re-echoed in all heads, namely that in a political constitution nothing should be recognized as valid unless its recognition accorded with the right of reason"* (281). Political restoration is thus for Hegel the pure antithesis of revolution; without any relation to the historical principle of the present, the restoration pits the past against it, and thereby makes this itself an empty form which historically has no real content left. Hegel therefore employed the sharpest words against the Wurtemberg Estates: they "like to spin words" (283); they act like a merchant "who proposed to ply his trade just the same on a ship, in which his capital was sunk, even though it had gone to the bottom, and to expect others to advance the same credit to him on the strength of it as before" (281). They have "forgotten nothing and learnt nothing"; for them the great experience of the age is all for nothing; they have "slept through the last twenty-five years, possibly the richest that world history has had, and for us the most instructive, because it is to them that our world and our ideas belong" (282). Therewith in Hegel's consideration of the false restoration, the positive meaning of his world-historical interpretation of the Revolution reveals itself; with the elevation of freedom as the universal principle of right, the Revolution has set before the age the task of making the Idea politically the content of law and state, which is from the start the principle and meaning of European world history. *Therefore, not the restoration, but the Revolution represents the principle of European history. For this reason, the political restoration suffers from an inner contradiction; its inverted character consists in that it opposes itself antithetically to the present-day principle and thus negates the historical substance itself, which it yet wishes to preserve and reestablish.* That necessarily entangles it in an empty formalism and ultimately condemns it to political impotence over and against the real problems of the age, which thereby remain unresolved.

The false restorative preservation is therefore for Hegel the real danger of the age; during his lifetime he never ceases considering it, and so in 1830 he takes it up one more time in his last writing, *On the English Reform Bill*,[25] in an examination of the English situation and the attempt to achieve a stable order through a reform of Parliament. The English possess a modern political constitution admired by many, they concern themselves with the reform and improvement of their parliamentary system. At the same time, however, they also ignore the transformed social relations and hold fast to outdated, obsolete, feudal prerogatives, privileges, and positive laws and thereby hazard the appearances of corruption resulting from the contradictions to reality. Where this occurs, however, all political transformations are necessarily condemned to inefficacy, if the tendency is not already overcome "to cling always to the old faith in the excellence of an institution, even if the present state of affairs derived from it is altogether corrupt" (298). The "cankers" (308) from which England politically suffers, are the "far too sharp a contrast" between the ruling positive laws and how the actual social relations of population, wealth, and interests have come to order themselves in modern times (298); it has led to a situation where England has fallen strikingly "behind the other civilized states of Europe in institutions derived from true rights" (300). This contradiction between the formality of positive law and the reality not identical with it is here as everywhere the problem whose solution must consist in "applying rational principles and introducing them to life as it is lived" (see HPW 326), if the denouement is not to be the continuation of revolution instead of sound reforms.

Thus, in Hegel's view, it is, philosophically as well as politically, a matter of drawing the revolutionary principle of right as freedom from out of the political struggle, and securing it against inundation by the storm of events in the ferment of the age. The political theory of 1821 takes it up and presupposes it as the thought and reason of the present. Where freedom becomes the basis of right, there the state must be conceived as "the actuality of concrete freedom" (PR par. 260). It becomes a state of right and exists as such when its individuals can be themselves as men, and "personal individuality and its particular interests . . . gain explicit recognition for their right . . . in the sphere of family and society" (par. 260). In this manner, "substantial freedom" gets posited as the sole ground and aim of state power. According to Hegel, all former foundations of the state are thereby annulled and corrected. It is no longer possible to attribute it to a "social impulse," a "desire of security for property . . . religious sentiment" or a "Divine appointment of the governing power" (PH 445–446). The rational principle of the Revolution has led beyond all these possibilities of foundation; they are annulled in its idea of right as freedom.

Thus philosophy pushes through the husk of appearances to the kernel, whose husk they are; it brings forth from the age itself the principle that drives on in the depths of the struggles of the day, in the conflict of opinion, and in the opposition of revolution and restoration, and seeks to become an historical shape.

III

6. Hegel's grappling with the French Revolution comes to a conclusion in the *Philosophy of Right,* and this conclusion consists of his adopting, in the theory of the state advanced therein, the freedom principle of the Revolution and understanding it as the presupposition of all coming legal and political orders. The youthful enthusiasm for the Revolution, which stands at the beginning of the philosophical path in Hegel's case, enters into his philosophy itself and continues on alive in its mature cast. His philosophy remains in the true sense a philosophy of revolution, in that it proceeds from it and draws life from it till the last. There is nothing in Hegel's intellectual development which marks it more than this positive relation to the Revolution; it determines its end as well as its beginning.

However, not only is the warding off of all restorative tendencies proper to it, but so, equally and no less unequivocally, is the critique of the Revolution itself, the fundamental insight into its inability to come to any viable constitution and give rise to firm, stable political and legal structures. Thus, to a certain degree, it can appear as if Hegel fell along his way between the fronts that formed in France, Germany, and elsewhere in Europe as an immediate result of the revolutionary movement. Nevertheless, the inner concern of Hegelian philosophy in its relation to the Revolution manifests itself in this external betweenness. For Hegel, the perennial driving on of the Revolution and the opposing restoration of the old belong together. The abstractness of the Revolution appears in their opposition. It is not two principles, two independent historical worlds, that stand anew opposed to one another after the Revolution. Rather, the restoration is itself the—essentially postrevolutionary—product of the Revolution. The restoration is founded upon the fact that the Revolution, in positing universal freedom in regard to man as man, simultaneously contains the contradiction of excluding from itself the historical substance of human existence and being its negation.[26]

In the same period in which Hegel progressively developed his philosophical position from enthusiasm to a theory of revolution, while dwelling in Bern and Frankfurt in a concentration isolating him from his friends, Novalis brought to completion his essay, *Christendom or Europe* (1799), which still today continues to have an effect in the romantic opposition against the modern world. It has the form of an historical study that turns longingly toward the Middle Ages as the premodern world. Insofar, however, as it celebrates it as the "beautiful, glorious times when Europe was a Christian land" (WW Wasmuth I, 279), the present gets determined in opposition to it as the loss of the beautiful life. It comes to an end with the new age. The holy gets set aside, the music of the universe is silenced, religion loses its political, peacemaking influence; the Revolution finally rips apart the bond which once held together the "one lord," the "numerous guilds," the "beautiful assemblies in the mystic churches" (279f.). With the modern age and in its revolution, the end of Christendom has become political reality and the fate of the epoch. Its "new belief" is "restlessly occupied with purging poetry from nature, the soil, the human soul, and the sciences—with eradicating every trace of the holy" (291).[27]

Three decades later, as Hegel for the last time delivered his lectures on the *Philosophy of History* and, in its framework, his interpretation of the Revolution as an epoch in the world-historical path of the Idea, Comte's *Positive Philosophy* begins to appear (1830). The "three-stage law" gets formulated as the great axiom of progress. With modern society and science, theology and metaphysics, and the "stages" of human development borne by them, become the historical past. Man, freed from their dominion and come into his own, progresses toward the consummation of humanity through modern science and society, and leaves behind him former history and its traditions as a dead historical past.[28]

Hegel knew neither Comte's thesis nor the romantic poeticization of the Middle Ages by Novalis, but the tendency that takes philosophical shape with both, the romantic restoration of the old and its overcoming through progress, is typical of the relation to one another in which the world of historical tradition and the new age with its future of progress have come to stand. They fall asunder; historical continuity tears apart; the new age becomes the end of former history; Novalis understands it as the downfall of the historical substance, Comte as the liberation of man from it.

Only with this does it become comprehensible what is meant by the fact that Hegel understands the freedom of the Revolution as the present, universalized form of the original metaphysical freedom of selfhood, and so conceives the revolution itself as a world-historical situation and as an epoch of the One World History whose principle is known and spiritually preserved in the tradition of the One Philosophy. Philosophical theory, which can appear externally as a taking up of the thread of speculation and its spinning out, that is, as the inner unfolding of philosophical thought into a system, proves itself to be the *settlement of the problem posed by the Revolution, that the continuity of world history no longer stands and is broken for it as well as for its restorative opponents. What emerges with the new age and with the revolution is for both the end of former history; the future has no relation to tradition.* Hegel's theory takes up the problem of this historical discontinuity; it raises the question of what signifies, underlies, and brings forth the interpretation of the present as the end of history, an interpretation decisive for the Revolution itself in the same way as for its opponents. Hegel does not, however, take the side of one or the other, but rather grasps the problem of this world-historical discontinuity in its full radicality. The romantic restorative dismissal of the new age and its revolution belongs together with the revolutionary emancipation from the historical tradition; they have the same foundation. Both have in common the conviction that "the ethical world is Godless" (PR 4); whereas for the revolutionary theory and its followers the present signifies the end of the old world and the liberation of man from what have become the "unreal" powers of religion and metaphysics. From the other side this identically recognized end of the historical tradition appears as the elimination of divinity from the world, as the loss of the true, the holy, and the beautiful, as the downfall of the humanness of man himself. *The revolutionary negation of the past and the restorative negation of the present are therefore identical in their presupposition of the historical discontinuity of tradition and future, and this discontinuity thus becomes for Hegel the decisive problem of the age; it goes unresolved in all the tensions and antagonisms of the period.* He takes it up and settles it philosophically, thereby exposing his philosophy itself—almost out of necessity—to dual misinterpretation as a reduction of the religious substance to what is political and historical, and as a reactionary idealistic veiling of the revolutionary liberation of man from theological and metaphysical heaven.

7. What takes place? What does Hegel achieve by relating the Revolution to the ancient-Christian freedom and its world history in order to conceive the revolution thus as the epoch of that freedom's universal political realization; and what does he gain by thereby holding up the continuity of world history against the negation of tradition by the Revolution as well as the negation of the present by the restoration and romantic philosophy, and thus the dichotomy of tradition and future presupposed by both?

Hegel attempted to interpret away neither this dichotomy

and its real power over men and their consciousness, nor the pain which fills the existence ensnared in it. For him, it is the fundamental condition of the modern age.

His philosophy proceeds out of suffering from it; the need for it originates in the dichotomy: "When the might of union vanishes from the life of men and the antitheses lose their living connection and reciprocity . . . the need of philosophy arises" (DFS 91); its "source" is the "dichotomy" (89); in its "fragmentation" lies the "confusion of the time" (178). At the start of his intellectual path, Hegel, like Schiller and Hölderlin, looks back upon the Greek world which still possessed the "ensouled unity" now lost in the dichotomy; "Alas, an image from the distant days of the past shines against the soul—the image of a genius of the peoples—a son of good fortune . . . We know of this genius only from hearsay, only a few traces of him have we been granted to regard with love and wonder in discarded copies of his figure which only awaken a painful longing for the original" (*Volksreligion*, Nohl, pp. 28f.). The present lives in the dichotomy; the lost unity is yearned for with ardent desire. The historical source of the dichotomy corresponds to this. As in the eyes of the poets, it appears as the work of the new age and its "enlightening understanding"; it is the fruit of its victory. Through it and its science, the divine universe gets transformed into dead, mechanical nature. The divine of tradition becomes alienated from reality; it gets transformed for the understanding "into the concept either of superstition or of entertainment" (DFS 92). Thereby the beautiful becomes a thing; the sacred grove becomes timber, the temple becomes "logs and stones"; the understanding excludes the divine from the objective reality it has reified. The thing is but a thing and has lot the connection with the overarching original meaning of existence. However, already in the writings of the Jena period there are indications of the insight that allows Hegel to bring to a positive determination the basis of the discontinuity and the problem underlying the notion of the end of world history. While the Enlightenment and the understanding make objective thinglike reality independent and absolute so that "the eternal remained in a realm beyond,"[29] subjectivity for Hegel belongs to, and is historically contemporaneous with, this "negative procedure" of "the Enlightenment" (56) and its reification of the world. Hegel calls it the "principle of the North, and from the religious point of view, of Protestantism" (57), in reference to the "western locality" of the formation of the Enlightenment (DFS 177); it supervenes with the Enlightenment as the other "great form of the world spirit" (FK 57). By virtue of this subjectivity, what the understanding had excluded from its objective, thinglike reality is taken up into the realm of historical existence; it preserves in "feelings and persuasions" the beauty and truth which the understanding abandons: "Religion builds its temples and altars in the heart of the individual. In sighs and prayers he seeks for the God whom he denies to himself in intuition, because of the risk that the intellect will cognize what is intuited as a mere thing, reducing the sacred grove to mere timber." (57). What was one in the old world, falls asunder in the new age; the divine and the worldly, being and the existent become independent over and against one another; what the understanding does not preserve, in that it "scrupulously distinguishes the objective from the subjective" as "what is accounted worthless and null," "the struggle of subjective beauty" seeks to safeguard, namely "to defend itself properly against the necessity through which the subjective becomes objective" (57).

In this manner, the dichotomy is understood by Hegel as the form of the modern world and its consciousness. Whereas, however, the subjectively held beautiful and true, and the thinglike finitude, are absolutely opposed and alienated from one another without any connection, as much for subjectivity as for the understanding and its concept of objective reality, *Hegel conceives their dichotomy in a positive sense, as the form in which their original unity historically maintains itself under the conditions of the modern world. The objective reality of the Enlightenment, and the safeguarding subjectivity, are tied to one another in a complementary manner*; subjectivity builds its altars in the heart *because* the objective world of the understanding lies at hand. What fall assunder as subjectivity and objectivity and stand independently in contradiction to one another, remain historically together in the form of dichotomy. Hegel has before his eyes what can be called the double-tracked character of modern intellectual history, in which there belongs together with Descartes' *Methode*, Pascal's *Logique du coeur*; with "veritas logica," "veritas aesthetica" (Baumgarten); with the scholar and his rational system, the aesthetic subjectivity of genius (Shaftesbury); with Newton's nature, the beautiful nature of aesthetic poetry and art; with the rationalism of pietism, the religion of feeling. In a similar manner Dilthey later also set next to the Enlightenment a subjective mystical development of spirit, to which he then related Hegel's philosophy (for example, *Jugendgeschichte Hegels*, 1905); whereas Dilthey, however, allows the two tendencies to run along next to one another, without posing the question of their relation and the basis of their dichotomy, Hegel conceives the dichotomy of historical existence into subjectivity and objectivity as the form in which its unity maintains itself and in which the modern world finds its corresponding shape.

Thus, shortly after 1800, with his first publication in Jena, Hegel comes to the decisive insight: *There is no possibility of escaping from the dichotomy by joining with one side or the other so as to make the opposing one vanish as something non-existent.* Subjectivity and objectivity are rather historically referred to one another; they are together the substantial total historical existence. Its totality is present in the form of dichotomy; philosophy has to conceive it as this "already present" entity (DFS 93) by positing the whole—"the Absolute"—in the dichotomy and conceiving it within this as the "might of union." Philosophy thus opposes itself to the "absolute fixity" of "the dichotomy" in order to mediate and reconcile the "rigidified" oppositions in their contradiction (91). Its task consists in "uniting these presuppositions" divided in the dichotomy of subjectivity and objectivity by positing "dichotomy in the Absolute, as its appearance"; by positing "the finite in the infinite, as life" (93–94).[30]

In this way, Hegel's philosophy proceeds from the dichotomy considered as the historical formative principle of the age; its theory provides him with the presuppositions which make it possible to settle the problem of political revolution and the discontinuity of tradition and future posited with it. For this settlement, however, a second step is important. Philosophy itself is directed to the analysis of the concrete historical process and is thereby led beyond the cultural form of the opposition between romantic subjectivity and the Enlightenment, to the problems which condition and bear this opposition along in the historical process itself. This begins in Bern, and with it the decisive turning point is reached that then also leads Hegel away from his friends and the ideal of his youth. In the same years in which his theory of the dichotomy was formed, Hegel began here to immerse himself in the most profound way in the questions of the concrete political, economic, legal, and social relations of the age, doing so in direct connection with the universal problems of the revolution. These studies are directly mirrored in the comments which he adds to his translation—appearing anonymously in Frankfurt in 1798—of the Waadter attorney Cart's *Confidential Letters concerning the Former Relations of Political Law of Waadtland (Pays de Vaud)*, which treats the oppression meted out since 1791 by the Bern aristocracy.[31] The purpose is, in the first place, to bring its "discite justiciam moniti" to mention in

Germany as well. At the same time Hegel adds the observation characterizing his relation to political reality, namely, that the appeal to feeling could make one "rather mistrustful of the credibility of the matter," and thus that for many it would perhaps be better served with the "dry exposition of accounts of deeds" and with proof "by documents" (prefatory note, Dok. 248).

Hegel's own contribution corresponds to this. He listed as clearly as possible all of the more relevant facts: the measures taken by Bern, the rights of the parsonages, financial relations, tariff rates, the proceedings of the penal courts, the system of billeting, the technique of oppression in general. And what now becomes important for Hegel reveals itself therein: the attentiveness to how the universal "actually" happens, how oppression "actually" works, in what legal forms and actions political struggle "actually" gets carried out. We also know, however, that Hegel's occupation with the Swiss situation did not remain an isolated case; at that same time he was just as deeply concerned with the social and economic problems of England, its Parliament, the history of the American Revolution, the reform of Prussian state law, questions of the execution of sentences, and other matters as well.[32] In this turn to the concrete historical affairs of the age of revolution, Hegel becomes aware that there are no possibilities of drafting and constructing in thought, from out of philosophical principles, ready universal solutions to the problems which play themselves out in historical reality. The problems of the Revolution, the dichotomy of existence, and the discontinuity of history for the culture of the age grounded in it, cannot be overcome in the speculative deduction of a new world that ought to be. History is itself the realm in which the Idea is actual and at work; the reason of the age is present in that which is, and theory has to bring it forth from the age itself as its concept. Since Hegel comes to realize this, and since philosophy itself then gets relegated to an insight into what is historically-concretely at hand, he encounters the decisive factor: *He becomes familiar with the social theory of English political economy.* At that time in Bern he read Steuart's *Inquiry into the Principles of Political Economy* (London 1767) and furnished it with a detailed running commentary.[33] In this study, the essence of civil society became clear to him, as Rosenkranz says (Rosenkranz, p. 86; Dok. 280); Hegel learned to comprehend the meaning of need and labor, the division of labor, the different capital of the classes, poverty, administration, and taxes; it dawns on him that *the historical essence of the Revolution and of the entire age and all its problems is the emergence of the modern industrial civil society of labor.*

Hardly even an echo of these studies and of the decisive spiritual turn bound up with them reached Hegel's friends at that time. Only hinting, Hegel alludes by letter to "works and studies," and that he would begin from the "subordinate needs of men" and shift his attention to the question of "what return to intervention in the life of men might be found" (Br. 29 to Schelling from Frankfurt on November 2, 1800).[34]

What actually took place, however, came out in the open in its full significance for Hegel's political philosophy twenty years later.[35] In the *Philosophy of Right* civil society has finally become the centerpoint; all political, legal, and spiritual problems of the age are referred to it as the epochal upheaval determining all, whose theory supersedes the consideration of the political revolution.

8. The depiction of civil society in the form in which Hegel develops it in the *Philosophy of Right* contains in the first instance no essentially new determinations in comparison to English political economy. Hegel conceives it in its unfolding as a "System of Needs"; it is that *society which—in a fundamental emancipation* *from all presuppositions of the historically bequeathed order of human life—has for its content solely the needful nature of man as an individual and its satisfaction in the form of abstract labor and the division of labor*; it contains according to its own principle nothing that is not posited by the "mediation of need and one man's satisfaction through his work and the satisfaction of the needs of all others" (PR par. 188). Those are in essence the basic concepts that Adam Smith (*An Inquiry into the Nature and the Causes of the Wealth of Nations*, London, 1776) had developed, which the *Philosophy of Right* also expressly refers to in addition to Say and Ricardo (PR par. 189). Whereas Hegel, when referring to the political theories of the Revolution, say to that of Rousseau, always at the same time also points critically to their abstractness and their fundamentally inadequate one-sidedness with respect to historical reality, he acts otherwise in his fastening upon *political economy*. The political theories of the Revolution, as deductive positings of new political forms from principles, have at the same time the immediate determination of making possible the revolutionary emancipation from the existing historical institutions and legal forms, and of destroying these in the positing of the new; therefore in principal they do not overcome the negativity in whose service they stand. In contrast to this, Hegel understood English political economy as the inductive (hermeneutical) theory of the already existing, historically constituted social reality, which seeks to extract from it the principles that determine it as its inner law. Therein lies, in Hegel's view, the pathbreaking significance and "honor" of this new science; in it, thought draws the principles from "the endless mass of details which confront it at the outset," and develops them thus as the "simple principles of the thing" from the relations in which they are active and which they govern (par. 189). The laws are discovered for a "mass of accidents." And then Hegel adds the significant observation that "one would least expect" to find these laws worked out by political economy, "because at first sight everything seems to be given over to the arbitrariness of the individual" (par. 189 Addition). Later, however, one sees that it is the same with modern society as with the planetary system, which also "displays to the eye only irregular movements, though its laws may none the less be ascertained" (*ibid.*). Smith and the other initiators of the new economic science have thus the same standing for the theory of civil society as Kepler has for the theory of planetary motion. They have discovered the laws that underly it and determine its formation. Thus Hegel adopts the theory of political economy and thereby connects it with philosophy for the first time, and not just for Germany. Since philosophy has the task of grasping its age in thought, it discovers in civil society the reality in which the Idea is historically existing at present.

This then becomes decisive for the philosophical consideration of the problem of political revolution, inasmuch as it too is necessarily tied to the transformations of historical life taking place with the emergence of civil society and must be understood in their context. Hegel knows that the determination decisive for the general understanding of the epoch and first worked out by political economy, lies in the foundation of society upon the concept of man's needful nature, insofar as through it, society's independence in principle from all pregiven historical presuppositions and therewith the emancipatory form of its constitution is established. This concept of needful nature therefore remains decisive for him as well; on it depend mediately or immediately all further basic concepts of society which he adopts, in connection with the principle of needful nature itself, from English theory. Individuals, as with Smith, are the subject of society, not in the totality of their historical, spiritual-ethical existence, but in restriction to what they are as bearers of production and consumption, in accord with the principle of needful nature. Correspondingly, society itself, in distinction from all former and hitherto existing societal and community forms, is also exclusively limited to those relations which connect individuals with one another in the satisfaction of need through labor. Therefore, as society, it is identical in Hegel's view to the "System of Needs." Thus it necessarily excludes all other relations from its sphere insofar as they do not belong to this system, with the result that the division of labor becomes the sole constitutive principle of society, as in the case of Adam Smith. The further determinations follow from this. Through the separation of the means of labor from the laboring individuals, a separation constitutive for the division of labor, society gets driven into "dependence and distress," and so becomes a class society in the dual process involving, on the one hand, the "amassing of wealth" and its concentration in a few hands, and on the other hand, the "subdivision and restriction of particular jobs . . . of the class tied to work of that sort" (par. 243). With "the standard of living of a large mass of people" falling "below a certain subsistence level," it produces "a rabble" (par. 244), which confronts the propertied class without mediation.[36]

Because, however, society stands at the same time under the law of rising production, the inner pressure intensifies and forces it into an expansion all over the earth: "When civil society is in a state of unimpeded activity, it is engaged in expanding internally in population and industry" (par. 243); its own "dialectic" drives it beyond itself (par. 246). It must seek consumers for the "goods it has overproduced" (compare par. 246) in other peoples and so enter upon the road of colonization (par. 248). Therefore, for Hegel the industrial, civil, class society is finally determined through its own law to become a world society; *the connection between freedom and humanity and man as species, which is decisive for the relation of political revolution to world history, is founded upon this potential universality of civil society.* Directly following Smith, Hegel states that the sea, being "the greatest means of communication," becomes its element; through trade and commerce it begins to integrate the most distant peoples into its sphere (par. 247).[37] In Hegel's view, it is endemic to this integration that at its end will also stand the dissolution of the colonial system; the freeing of the colonies will one day prove to be "of the greatest advantage to the mother country," just as already the emancipation of slaves now serves to the immediate favor of their masters (par. 248 Addition).

9. Thus with the *Philosophy of Right*, where Hegel follows in the footsteps of classical political economy, civil society finally steps into the center of philosophy and its political theory, where it is conceived as the potentially universal society of labor spreading out across the globe. While Schelling more and more casts aside every tie to the political and social problems of the Revolution upon which the friendship of his youth with Hegel primarily rested, and while Fichte—entangled in the narrowness of the German situation, and himself provincial through and through— deduces and postulates *a priori* state and legal systems out of his own head as "absolute Ego," for Hegel modern civil society becomes the all-determining problem which philosophical thought cannot ignore if it wants to conceive the existing reason and substance of the age in what is, and not lose itself in mere opining and sketchy imagining. This becomes decisive for his consideration of the French Revolution. For now it has become clear to Hegel in his encounter with political economy that *the political revolution itself and with it its central idea of freedom belong historically to the emergence of the new society; this is its actuality and historical necessity*. Freedom for all is its constitutive condition, insofar as it has for its subject individuals in the equality of their needful nature, and thus extricated from all institutions limiting them politically or legally (guilds, bondage, confinement to a

locality, privileges, etc.). The same thing follows from social labor; as labor, it presupposes the free being of individuals, because it is based upon their acting in their own interest and for their own sake and thus standing as free elements in the division of labor's process of production; freedom therefore has to count as its principle.[38] This insight, which already had axiomatic significance for political economy and its theory of society, is fully adopted by Hegel in the *Philosophy of Right*. Although he also sees that the principle of labor burdens society with the problems of class formation and the rise of the working class, and although he comprehends their full import and fateful significance, he nevertheless has seen the positive character of modern labor in this its constitutive connection with freedom, which lifts it beyond all former historical forms of social practice: "subsistence" that is received "directly, not by means of . . . work," and unfree labor are opposed to the "principle of civil society and the feeling of individual independence and self-respect in its individual members" (par. 245). With civil society, the "private persons whose end is their own interest" (par. 187) become citizens (citoyen) and subjects of modern society by way of labor, and Hegel can expressly call the free individual the "son of civil society" (par. 238).

In this way the revolutionary idea of the freedom of all is founded in the emergence of modern labor society; it is its necessary presupposition and the condition of its possibility, so that, in Hegel's view, its philosophical and political determination has to adhere to what it socially signifies and is, as civil freedom existing in the context of the social order posited by labor and the division of labor.

This becomes decisive. For Hegel, the unresolved state of the political problems of the Revolution is connected with the fact that its freedom, comprising its positive world-historical content, is saddled with the contradiction of dichotomy; its positing encompasses for itself the opposition against all historically pre-given orders and the old historical world; its political realization should usher in the end of former history. Owing to this discontinuity toward history, Hegel calls the freedom of the Revolution a "negative," an "abstract" freedom. Its negativity renders it a "fury of destruction." It drives it into self-destruction and at the same time summons as its antithesis the powers of restoration which, in opposition to the end of Western history arising with the Revolution, call back the old world and seeks its renewal, in order to undo the Revolution and so save the historical substance of man. The political constitution of freedom through the Revolution thus stands under the law of dichotomy; this is the basic condition of the age. Hegel proceeded from it in the five years from 1795 to 1800, which were decisive for the formation of his philosophy; against the reified objectivity of the understanding and the culture of the Englightenment, subjectivity seeks in sentiment and feeling to save the reality of the beautiful, true, and holy, which has been ruled out and set free by the understanding. Already with his insight into this dialectical unity of subjectivity and objectivity, Hegel had attained a position which enabled him to conceive the dichotomy and discontinuity in a positive way, as the form of historical continuity and unity. However, at the same time the indeterminacy still lingers on that the rational reification of reality appears as a misfortune and as an irruption of a force hostile to the substantial unity of historical life, and that subjectivity detaches from objective reality what it preserves, as a subjective factor belonging to pure inwardness, thereby turning it into something unreal which has lost every relation to the objective world. Therein lies the inner limit of the subjective reconciliation in all its forms, such that the problem of dichotomy itself and its positive historical meaning remains open. *Hegel is led beyond this form of inner reconciliation through the theory of civil society; it brings the decisive turn and opens to Hegel the way to the positive interpretation of the dichotomy itself and the objectivity driving it forward.*

The concept of nature of political economy has, in the same sense as all natural-right theories of law or state in the seventeenth and eighteenth centuries, the methodological purpose of guaranteeing against any adoption of concepts and principles belonging to the historically preceding orders and their metaphysical and theological theories, so that modern society can then stand as the immediate appearance of a human nature independent of history and constant over and against all historical transformations. Hegel understands, on the contrary, that this nature, constant and therefore ahistorical for economic theory, is the historical mark of civil society and expresses its emancipation from preceding historical orders and thereby its constitution through emancipation. Therefore, in the *Philosophy of Right*, the nature principle of society taken over from political economy is understood at the same time as the *historical* principle of society's emancipatory constitution. It enters into history as the power of differentiation, as "difference," and separates the historical formations of the family and the state from the social being of man. It steps "between them" and "splits" them apart by breaking out of this context and thus socially freeing the existence of the individual from the ethical and religious determinations it formerly bore in history (see pars. 182, 184 Addition). In accord with this, all other nature concepts of society, need and its satisfaction, and work and the division of labor, which Hegel adopts, remain "abstract" concepts for him; they entail the detaching of society and its practice from the history of tradition. Man thus certainly also remains for Hegel the subject of society in the sense of political economy, that is, as the producer and consumer who pursues the satisfaction of his need and labor, seeking to maintain and increase his prosperity. At the same time, however, this means in his view that society confines itself to the needful nature of man and disengages its practice from its historical context. Only when this disengagement is presupposed can man be understood in the social sense as laborer, producer, or consumer, without reference to what he otherwise is. With this insight Hegel has taken the decisive step beyond the theory of political economy. *He conceives the foundation of society upon nature as the form in which society makes itself independent over and against the history of tradition by emancipating itself from it. The ahistorical nature of society is its historical essence*; Hegel was the first to understand this;[39] and in doing so, he engendered the possibility of posing and resolving the problem of emancipation, insofar as it turns out that the problems of dichotomy and historical discontinuity stirring the age derive from the emergence of society and are posited through its emancipatory constitution. One can say still more: In Hegel's view, the essence of modern political revolution, which differentiates it from all other forms of upheaval, uprising, rebellion, and putsch, lies not so much in the particular political form which the violence takes, but rather in the social emancipation underlying it and in the establishment of an order that according to its own principle is presuppositionless, excluding everything preexisting, historical and traditional, like a radical new beginning that nothing should precede. Thus in all its forms, this revolution of emancipation ultimately has its source for Hegel in civil society; in reality this is itself the revolution which calls all into question and brings everything into a state of flux through an immediate alteration of concrete human existence more profound and incisive than any political transformation; and this is true even where—as in England—it comes to pass without political upheaval.

So it emerges for Hegel that society is also the driving force of political revolution; it brings dichotomy into history, but not within a partial sphere of human life in which man can still evade the new (as one can spiritually resist the culture of Enlightenment), but rather as the reality of human existence in its practical fulfillment which determines present and future. Thereby it becomes the unavoidable fate of all. Nonetheless, the social foundation of the emancipation reveals what the dichotomy and the abstract ahistoricality posited by it signify and realize *in a positive sense.* The abstract negativity against history is the final word as much for the theory of revolution as for that of restoration. Contrary to this, the social emancipation contains the positive determination that what it detaches from the context of historical tradition and makes independent over and against it, is the "System of Needs." *In the emancipation, society restricts itself to the natural sphere of human existence, to the satisfaction of need through labor and to the "natural will" of man, and thereby releases its other life relationships. The abstractness of society is identical in substance to this restriction to man's needful nature and sets free therewith the life relationships which are not reducible to it.* Therefore, for Hegel, man as subject of civil society is "abstract" man, detached from his historical and spiritual relationships and left standing in the equality of this needful nature. Whereas man is in abstract right a "person," in moral relationships a "subject" (in the Kantian sense), and in the family, on the other hand, a "family member," "here at the standpoint of needs . . . is the first time, and indeed properly the only time" (as Hegel adds with emphasis) we speak of "the composite idea which we call *man*" (par. 190). In civil society man counts because he is a man and not because he is a Jew, Catholic, Protestant, German, Italian, etc. (par. 209); therefore the orders of his historical heritage which are decisive for his own existence, do not play a role in society. On this rests the abstractness and ahistoricality of the human existence posited through it, which also determines the political theory of revolution and its negative idea of freedom. At the same time, however, this abstractness in the sphere of

society is characterized by its restriction to the natural relationships of human existence and man's satisfaction of need
through labor. Therein lies its positive significance, and Hegel
can therefore say that society has for its content "subjectivity"
only "in its natural subjective embodiment, that is, in needs, inclinations, passions, opinions, fancies, etc." (par. 123). Its aim
lies, as is stated following political economy, solely in the "welfare" (wealth, happiness)* of men; it therefore touches only
their outer, natural existence; it is identical to the "ends of the
whole sphere of finitude" (par. 123) and thus excludes from the
social order all determinations of the person and private existence which encroach upon welfare. *Because it has only the "natural will" for its content, it therefore releases to it the "true determinations
of freedom" and its selfhood. In this lies the positive historical meaning
of abstract freedom and its emancipatory constitution through the dichotomy.* Because the end of society is exclusively the "welfare"
of man, no ends are posited by it which would annul the right
of particularity and with it, the substantial freedom of man. Society grants subjectivity the right of particularity precisely
through its abstract ahistoricality.

Thus in the analysis of civil society and its principle of needful
nature, it becomes clear to Hegel that the dichotomy not only
does not have to lead to the destruction of world-historical continuity, but is precisely the condition that makes it possible and
can secure the continuance of the substantial order of tradition
within the realm of the modern world. *Existing reason reveals itself
in the present not in the inner preservation of subjectivity in its antitheti-
cal relation to social and political revolution, but in the dichotomy making it possible.* The world-historical meaning of revolution lies for
Hegel in the thought that freedom is the right of all men. Its
realization, however, makes necessary the emancipation of soci-

*These two words are given in English by Ritter.

ety from the historical presuppositions of tradition. It becomes universal because it sets outside itself the historical determination of man and what differentiates men as members of different peoples and in the variety of their spiritual and religious ancestry. It can encompass all men as men in the equality of their needful nature and abstract labor. Nevertheless, the dichotomy belongs to it; therefore, for Hegel, this is at the same time in a positive sense the reason why the ahistorical abstractness necessarily constitutive for society itself cannot lead to a decisive settlement of its contradiction with history, nor thus to an abolition of the freedom of selfhood and the historical substance essential to it.

Whereas the nature theory of society, as Hegel adopts it from political economy, leaves its relation to history unexamined, Hegel has treated its problem philosophically. The present in all spheres of inner and outer life is determined through the social and political revolution; no philosophical theory can ignore this presupposition. However, it can nonetheless be understood as an epoch of world history. What alone saves the continuity of world history and its spirit is not subjectivity with its inner preservation. It is rather society's form of dichotomy itself, since in its limitation to man's needful nature and to the objective thing-like reality of subjectivity belonging to it, society allows for the right of subjectivity's particularity and its freedom, and thus leaves open the possibility of its preservation.

For Hegel, this also signifies that civil society itself does not *historically* consist in its singular restriction to its own natural principle, but rather presupposes its place in the entire formation of man which has been molded in the world-historical labor of reason, without its own theory, based solely on the natural principle, being able to maintain this place and bring it to verbal expression. Hegel's philosophy must therefore go beyond it; while he on the one hand conceives the emergence of civil soci-

ety and the revolution coming to pass with it from out of civil
society's own natural principle, he on the other hand relates society at the same time to the knowledge of the rational substance
of all world history preserved in the philosophical tradition.
Reference is made to it at the end of the *Philosophy of Right.* As
the "element in which the universal mind exists" and "the actuality of mind in its whole compass of internality and externality
alike" (par. 341), it remains necessarily left out of account in
political economy and its theory of society, since the latter must
bracket out and abstract from everything historical in the development of the inner principle of society and its laws of motion.
Against this, however, philosophy can develop in a positive way
the relation to historical origins that is posited with its emancipatory constitution, but allowed to disappear in the nature-
bound theory. In this manner, philosophy is led to conceive the
emancipation as dichotomy. With this, society itself and its revolution become explainable in a positive manner within the context of world history. For its part, it can count as "the movement
of mind" (par. 341) and as the sphere of ethical life's appearance
(compare par. 181).

The *Philosophy of Right*'s theory of the state has then the task
of completing what has become the necessary correction of the
nature-bound theory of society. The latter cannot go beyond the
system of needs and the society posited through it, and must
remain standing before what Hegel calls the abstract "state
based on need, the state as the Understanding envisages it" (par.
183). Hegel's doctrine of the state as "reality of the ethical Idea"
and as "spirit that realizes itself in the world"—which contains
the determinations that then lead to the condemnation of his
philosophy as reactionary and as a deification of the state—has
the methodological task of validating the historical substance of
modern society and of grasping in their concept those determinations which cannot be won from their abstract natural and

emancipatory principle, without connection to the historical substance.[40]

10. In this manner, Hegel's theory of society and of the revolution arising with it becomes philosophical theory; the speculative concept becomes necessary in view of the abstractness constitutive for society itself; concealed in it lies the danger that society can come to make its labor- and class-system the sole determination of man. When this happens, and when the emancipation principle is thus elevated to an absolute power, and all that man is independently of society is not set free but really negated, then society must actually step out of the realm of world history and come to its end. Hegel was aware of this possibility of an absolute socialization of man and thus of the elimination of the dichotomy by it: "Civil society is . . . the tremendous power which draws men into itself and claims from them that they work for it, *owe everything to it, and do everything by its means*" (par. 238 Addition—emphasis Ritter's).

This danger becomes acute when society, "in a state of unimpeded activity, . . . is engaged in expanding internally" (see par. 243) and so ousting from itself and annihilating the powers of private life, subjectivity, and tradition, which are set free in the dichotomy and implicitly preserved historically. Where the genuine civil life of the person, sure in its sphere, ceases to be a "hard ground," there grows the "danger to individuals, society, and the state . . . just as a spark falling on a heap of gunpowder is more dangerous than if it falls on hard ground where it vanishes without trace" (par. 319). In this sense, Hegel, at the end of his life, foresaw future possibilities of continuing revolution, and called the Revolution itself the problem that will be passed on unresolved to coming ages.

For this reason, the "Godless" state of the "ethical world" must appear to him as a sign of the most extreme danger, insofar as it comprises what the restorative, romantic subjectivity represents it to be, namely an ethical atheism taking the potentiality, the social reality of man, to be godless and accordingly condemning it as the end and demise of the history of tradition. The historical character of modern society rests upon the fact that it sets free in the form of dichotomy the substance preserved in subjectivity and thereby contains it as the living content of the freedom it has posited.

When, however, the subjective sensibility seeks to rescue the divine from it, society therewith gets stripped of the substance which it historically bears. The powers maintaining it are destroyed; the rescue itself calls into being the demise it wishes to forestall. This deadly danger confronted Hegel. He withstood it by seeking and finding reason presently existing not just in his own inner life and beyond the age, but in the historical movement and its process of formation, in the political and social revolution, and in its contradictory appearance which has become the fate of the modern age in general.

Notes

1. The *Philosophy of Right* is cited in its paragraph divisions following the "new critical edition" of Hegel's works (Hegel's *Sämtliche Werke*, edited by Joh. Hoffmeister, vol. XII, Hamburg 1955). Since Hoffmeister has removed from the text the additions (*Zusätze*) contained in the edition of Gans, and reserved their publication for a separate volume (see the forward of the fourth edition, pp. xiiff.) which has not yet appeared, the additions are cited following the Stuttgart edition, vol. VII.

The political writings are quoted from the text of the *Schriften zur Politik und Rechtsphilosophie*, Leipzig 1923, edited by G. Lasson, so far as they are *not* included in the Stuttgart edition or the new critical edition. References from the *"Beurteilung der im Druck erschienenen Verhandlungen in der Versammlung der Landstände des Königsreichs Württemberg im Jahre 1815 und 1816"* (*Proceedings of the Estates Assembly in the Kingdom of Wurtemberg*) and from the writing *Über die englische Reformbill* (*The English Reform Bill*) are taken from the Stuttgart edition, vol. VI, and from the *Berliner Schriften 1818–1831* (Neue Kritische Ausgabe, vol. XI, Hamburg 1956) edited by Hoffmeister, respectively. Quotations from the *Jugendschriften* (Tübingen, Bern, Frankfurt) are based upon *Hegels theologische Jugendschriften*, edited by H. Nohl, Tübingen 1906, and Hoffmeister's collection of *Dokumente zu Hegels Entwicklung* (Dok.), Stuttgart 1936.

Passages of letters are quoted following the consecutive numbering of Hoffmeister in his critical edition of the *Briefe von und an Hegel* (Br.): vol. I, letters from 1785–1812, 1952; vol. II, letters from 1813–1822, 1953; vol. III, letters from 1823–1831, 1954.

All other writings are taken from the Stuttgart edition, to which the volume numbers added to the titles refer so far as they do not appear in the volumes of the "Philosophischen Bibliothek" edited by Hoffmeister after 1949.

Some comments to this essay have been placed at its end as an Appendix. [This Appendix is included in the present work, following these notes.] Concerning the handling of a bibliography of Hegel's political philosophy see Appendix, sec. I.

2. Rudolf Haym, *Vorlesungen über Hegel und seine Zeit*, Berlin 1857.

3. Haym's lectures presuppose the Young Hegelians' critique of Hegel before 1848 and summarize it in essence; whereby, however, the problems of civil society strongly recede into the background and the significance of emancipation is seen above all in the emergence of the positive sciences and in the overcoming of theology and metaphysics through them. Löwith therefore observes that Haym subjects the "motifs of attack" of the Young Hegelians to an "academic modification" (see *From Hegel To Nietzsche*, Doubleday, New York 1967, p. 57). A good first survey of the critique of Hegel and its history is provided by W. Moog, *Hegel und die Hegelsche Schule* (*Gesch. d. Philos. in Einzeldarstellungen* sec. VII, vol. 32/33, Munich 1930, pp. 438–487). One finds the basic presentation of the philosophical consideration of Hegel in the above-mentioned book of Löwith (pp. 63ff.) For the history of Hegel's political philosophy, besides E. Weil's out-

standing studies on Hegel's state theory (*Hegel et L'Etat*, Paris 1950), reference can be made to H. Marcuse, *Reason and Revolution: Hegel and the Rise of Social Theory*, London 1955, to Sidney Hook, *From Hegel to Marx* (Studies in the Intellectual Development of Karl Marx), London 1936 (Hook views Hegel's theory from the standpoint of its—for Hook, "necessary"—overcoming by Marx), to Vaughan, *Studies in the History of Political Thought before and after Rousseau*, vol. II, From Burke to Mazzini, edited by A. G. Little, Manchester 1939, chap. IV, pp. 143–183, and finally to G. H. Sabine, *A History of Political Theory*, New York 1937, 1950, pp. 620ff. Particularly rich in material is also H. Hirsch, *Denker und Kämpfer*, Gesammelte Beiträge zur Geschichte der Arbeiterbewegung, Frankfurt/Main 1955 (treating both Hilgards, as well as K. J. Köppen, Moses Hess, Marx, and Jaurès).

4. See Appendix sec. II.

5. See Appendix sec. III.

6. Concerning the Logic, understood as Hegel's metaphysics, see H. Hartmann, *Hegel*, 1929, pp. 143ff. See further Hegel's *Science of Logic* trans. by A. V. Miller, Humanities Press, New York 1976, p. 63): "The objective logic, then, takes the place rather of former *metaphysics* which was intended to be the scientific construction of the world in terms of *thoughts* alone"; as well as the *Encyclopedia* (*Hegel's Logic*, trans. by William Wallace, Oxford 1975, p. 36): "Logic therefore coincides with Metaphysics."

7. Compare in detail in this regard J. Ritter, "Die Lehre vom Ursprung und Sinn der Theorie bei Aristoteles" (in J. Ritter, *Metaphysik und Politik*, Frankfurt am Main 1969, pp. 9ff.).

8. G. W. F. Hegel, *The Difference Between Fichte's and Schelling's System of Philosophy*, trans. by H. S. Harris and Walter Cerf, State University of New York Press, Albany 1977, p. 87: "If the Absolute, like Reason which is its appearance, is eternally one and the same—as indeed it is—then every Reason that is directed toward itself and comes to recognize itself, produces a true philosophy and solves for itself the problem which, like its solution, is at all times the same . . . with respect to the inner essence of philosophy there are neither predecessors nor successors." In the same sense, see the *Enzyklopädie* (1817), pars. 7 and 8 (VI, 25). The basis for this unity of all philosophies, which permits one to speak of "philosophies" (in the plural), lies in the identity of their object, the absolute or being, understood as "not . . . what is gone, but . . . the living present" (G. W. F. Hegel, *Lectures On The History of Philosophy*, trans. by E. S. Haldane and F. H. Simson, Humanities Press, New York 1968, vol. I, p. 39). In distinction from the traditional idea of philosophia perennis, the One Philosphy in Hegel's view is, as such, historical at the same time; its intrinsically identical "eternal Being" (vol. I, p. 39; "which moths cannot corrupt, nor thieves break through and steal") consists in the variety of shapes which philosophy passes through historically, so that the One Philosophy as a whole is at the same time philosophy in its entire history.

Notes

It is the "universal Mind presenting itself in the history of the world in all the richness of its form" (vol. I, p. 33).

9. The *Philosophy of History*, trans. by J. Sibree, Dover, New York 1956, pp. 445 and 447, shows well how indissolubly political theory and philosophy are linked together in Hegel. There the "intellectual principle" of the French Revolution is set in immediate relation to the principle of reason of ancient philosophy: "Anaxagoras had been the first to say that νοῦς governs the World; but not until now had man advanced to the recognition of the principle that Thought ought to govern spiritual reality." For Hegel, the reason of revolution is identical with the reason of traditional philosophy; it gets politically realized in the French Revolution. Therefore if one removes Hegel's political theory from philosohy and leaves out of consideration the metaphysical origins and significance of its basic concepts, then one necessarily misinterprets his political theory; one transforms and destroys it, just as one conversely empties Hegel's philosophy and robs it of its substance when one takes it out of its relation to history and to the political and social problems of the age and understands it as a system which lays down thoughts from out of itself in pure thinking.

10. Nietzsche, Musarion edition, XVI, 82.

11. See Appendix sec. IV.

12. *Hegel's Political Writings*, translated by T. M. Knox, Oxford 1964, p. 330.

13. See Appendix sec. V.

14. See Appendix sec. VI.

15. G. W. F. Hegel, *Phenomenology of Spirit*, translated by A. V. Miller, Oxford, New York 1977, p. 355.

16. E. Gans in his foreword to the *Philosophy of Right*, VII, 6f.: "What, however, did one find, who despite the outcry and its hissing dissemination, came closer and entered? Did not he find the entire work erected out of a metal of freedom, did he find any resisting pull, any backward movement, paying homage to the Middle Ages in the relations of today and having nothing to say to the present age?"

17. Aristotle, *Metaphysics*, I, 2; 982b25f.: ἄνθρωπος . . . ἐλεύθερος ὁ αυτοῦ ἕνεκα καὶ μὴ αλλου ὤν.

18. Compare J. Ritter, "Das bürgerliche Leben. Zur aristotelischen Theorie des Glücks" (*Metaphysik und Politik*, pp. 57ff.).

19. *Philosophy of History*, p. 452: "We have . . . to consider the French Revolution in its organic connection with the *History of the World*; for in its substantial import

that event is World-Historical, and that contest of Formalism which we discussed in the last paragraph must be properly distinguished from its wider bearings."

20. See Appendix sec. VII.

21. See Appendix sec. VIII.

22. Th. Schieder has pointed out that the standardbearers of the political restoration, Metternich, de Maistre, and v. Haller, among others, saw the Revolution not, like Hegel, as the appearance of an objective historical crisis, but as the result of a conspiracy and poisoning of society (*Das Problem der Revolution im 19. Jahrhundert*, Hist. Zs. 170, 1950, pp. 243f.). In an analogous sense Vaughan also notes (Vaughan II, 178) that whereas Burke viewed the revolution in blind hate, Hegel kept himself free of such passion, "which distorted the vision of Burke."

Concerning the philosophy of restoration, see R. Spaemann, *De Bonald und die Philosophie der Restauration*, diss. Münster 1952 (published under the title: *Der Ursprung der Soziologie aus dem Geiste der Restauration. Studien über L. G. A. de Bonald*, Munich 1959).

23. The proceedings in Wurtemberg to which the *Proceedings of the Estates Assembly in the Kingdom of Wurtemberg* refer, are presented in detail by Rosenzweig (II, 33ff.).

Compare further E. Hölzle, *Das alte Recht und die Revolution (1784–1815), Munich 1931; and by the same author, König Friedrich von Württemberg*, in Württ. Vjhefte f. Landesgesch., N.F. 36.

24. Niethammer's letter of December 27, 1817 (Br. 327): "I would like to wager that you would not write your review if you were in a position, I am, to see this ruling reason face to face! For this reason, however, my thanks for this review are no less sincere. The least that I know to say about it is that it handles an awful matter in an intelligent way." In his letter of response of January 31, 1818, Hegel justified his "distribution of presents to our fathers of the people" with the remark, characteristic of Hegel's basic attitude, that he knows of nothing worse than "when one turns something good, indeed something most noble, into something worse through lack of understanding" (Br. 329).

Haym, it should be added, ascribed to this writing "self-seeking motives," namely that Hegel sought to promote himself as a candidate for the Tübingen chancery office. Haym then later retracted this accusation in his *Erinnerungen aus meinem Leben*, Berlin 1902, p. 257 (see on this point Hoffmeister, n. 4 to Br. 327, vol. II, p. 423).

25. The essay appeared first in the official Prussian state newspaper in installments (March 26th, 27th, and 29th), then, however, its further publication was interrupted, certainly through the efforts of the King; on this see Lasson in the preface to his edition of Hegel's political writings (1923, p. xxvi), further Rosenzweig (II, 225ff.). From his time in Bern on, Hegel always continued to concern

himself with the political relations and institutions of England; H. Höhne's *Hegel und England*, in: Kant-Studien XXXVI, pp. 301–326, is instructive on this matter.

In 1830, under the direct influence of the July Revolution, the opposition in England won an election victory that led to the fall of the Tory cabinet of Welington; with this, the path was laid open for the attempts at reform, the course of which Hegel's writing traces. With regard to the course that matters took in detail, see Rosenzweig (II, 225ff.), and in addition, G. M. Trevelyan, *History of England*, London 1945–1947, pp. 630ff. Trevelyan describes above all the manifestations of social crisis that lead urgently to reform; see also B. Guttman, *England im Zeitalter der bürgerlichen Reform*, Stuttgart 1949 (pp. 382ff.); Guttman judges Hegel's writing very negatively and dismisses it as a "disagreeable treatise" ruined "by a haughty lack of understanding" which "enlists higher reason for the authoritarian German type" (*ibid.*, p. 437).

26. In a manner similar to Hegel, Goethe understood the "historical consciousness of Romanticism" and its "polemic against modernity" as an antithesis to the "modern optimism of progress" of the French Revolution and liberalism. Therefore Goethe also considered both to be "thoroughly related or even identical in essence." See Kl. Ziegler, *Zu Goethes Deutung der Geschichte*, DV j. f. Lit. wiss. u. Geistegesch. XXX, 1956 (Kluckhohn-Festschrift), p. 262. See in addition H. J. Schrimpf, *Das Weltbild des späten Goethe, Überlieferung und Bewahrung in Goethes Alterswerk*, Stuttgart 1956, particularly pp. 126ff., 183ff., 251ff., and 294ff; Cl. Heselhaus, *Zur Idee der Widerherstellung*, DV j. XXI, 1951, pp. 54ff.; Sengle, *Voraussetzungen und Erschienungen der deutschen Restaurationsliteratur*, DV j. XXX, 1956, pp. 268ff.

27. See Appendix sec. IX.

28. See Appendix sec. X.

29. G. W. F. Hegel, *Faith and Knowledge*, translated by Walter Cerf and H. S. Harris, State University of New York Press, Albany 1977, p. 56.

30. See Appendix sec. XI.

31. Concerning the history of the origins of this work, its sources, and its publication, see in addition to Rosenzweig (I, pp. 51ff.) and Haering (I, pp. 292ff.), Hoffmeister, *Dokumente* (pp. 457ff.).

32. Concerning Hegel's political-historical studies in Bern, see besides Rosenzweig (I, 30ff.) and Haering (I, 124f.), also F. Bülow, *Die Entwicklung der Hegelschen Sozialphilosophie*, Leipzig 1920, pp. 20ff.; H. Höhne, *Hegel und England*, in Kant-Studien XXXVI, 1931, pp. 301ff.

According to Haering (I, pp. 16ff.), the "insatiable hunger for facts and bits of information . . . in the field of cultural history, including geography and ethnology" is already characteristic of Hegel the schoolboy, as his excerpts and

Hegel and the French Revolution

diaries prove. Haering just as much stresses Hegel's early interest in "supra-individual cultural phenomena such as civil society, law, state, religion, church, etc." (*ibid.*).

The encounter with Montesquieu is what above all stands behind these interests (in this regard, see in addition to the works cited above, H. Trescher, *Montesquieus Einfluss auf die philosophischen Grundlagen der Staatslehre Hegels*, diss., Leipzig 1920). What is decisive, however, is that all these historical-political interests do not remain isolated, but are connected with philosophy, and so give direction to the development of the latter, in that they refer it to the concrete historical reality. That leads Hegel's philosophy beyond Fichte and Schelling and beyond every form of deductive idealism.

33. In addition to the Tübingen translation published by Cotta 1769–1772, which Hegel probably used (see Dok. p. 466), there simultaneously appeared a second German translation in Hamburg edited by J. v. Pauli (2 volumes, 1769).

Regarding Hegel's commentary see Hoffmeister (Dok. p. 466). Rosenkranz (*G. W. F. Hegels Leben*, Berlin 1844, p. 85, reprinted in Dok. p. 280) still knew of it and remarked that "it is still preserved in its entirety." The significance that the study of English political economy has for Hegel's philosophy is something that, in addition to P. Vogel, *Hegels Gesellschaftsbegriff*, Berlin 1925 (pp. 115ff.), Lukàcs (*op. cit*) above all has now shown; however, Rosenzweig (II, p. 120) also stresses that Hegel views economic life "with the eyes of the classical political economy of the West," admittedly without clearly comprehending the constitutive significance of this connection for Hegel's political philosophy. Furthermore, Hamann had already studied Stewart in depth: "Stewart's political economy is a fine work full of great philosophical profundity . . . He says in two words more than Ferguson does in an entire chapter" (*Briefwechsel*, ed. Ziesemer/Henkel, vol. II, Wiesbaden 1956, p. 418).

34. The letter is particularly important because it shows how through his Bern studies, Hegel is led away from Schelling and manages to go beyond the idea of a philosophical revolution derived from Fichte (see Br. 11). Schelling had already in 1796 strongly urged Hegel to take up "also in public the good cause" (Br. 16 of January 1796) and reproached him for his "indecision": "Permit me to say one thing more to you! You seem to be currently in a state of indecision . . . and of even disheartenment which is totally unworthy of you" (Br. 17 of June 20, 1796). Hegel's letter from Frankfurt then shows what really occurred in the Bern period. Hegel went beyond the "ideal of his adolescence" and was "driven into science" (Br. 29). Hegel's remark about intervening in the life of men is to be referred to this turn of philosophy itself, a remark which announces, according to Löwith (p. 180), intention of going to the university; see on the contrary W. R. Beyer (p. 281, n. 36).

35. See Appendix sec. XII.

36. See Appendix sec. XIII.

37. What the sea signifies for modern society, and what the opposition of sea and

land has meant for world history and the formation of the tensions moving it on, are matters that C. Schmitt has presented with great mastery and with a profound understanding of the spiritual relationships and background which are here at play (see *Der Nomos der Erde*, 1950, pp. 144ff.; *Land und Meer*, Stuttgart 1954 Reclam UB, Number 7536). C. Schmitt expressly refers to Hegel's significance in this area (*Nomos der Erde*, p. 20, in addition: *Die geschichtliche Struktur des heutigen Weltgegensatzes von Ost und West*, in *Freundschaftliche Begegnungen, Festschrift für Ernst Jünger zum 60. Geburtstag*, Frankfurt/Main 1955, pp. 135–167, on Hegel pp. 164f.).

38. See Appendix sec. XIV.

39. K. Marx adopts this insight, first gained by Hegel, into the historical character of the "nature" of civil society; it becomes decisive for Marx's critique of political economy, so far as it involves unmasking the natural constants of English political economy as fictions and eliminating them historically. See for example, the *Grundrisse*, New York, 1973, pp. 83f.

40. See Appendix sec. XV.

Appendix to
Hegel and the
French Revolution

I

A bibliography on Hegel's political theory encounters difficulties connected with the peculiarity of Hegelian philosophy and of the history of its influence and interpretation.

The *Philosophy of Right* can certainly be understood as the great compendium of Hegel's political and social theory; however, that does not mean that it is limited to the sphere of political and social problems. Herein lies the difficulty: The political theory presupposes philosophical relationships which point beyond itself. Thus, the object of the *Philosophy of Right* is, as the Introduction (par. 33) states, freedom determined as the "development of the Idea of the absolutely free will," and indeed such that "abstract right," "morality," and "ethical life" are handled one after another, whereby the state falls under the concept of ethical life together with the family and civil society. With its linkage of law and ethical life (morality), this writing stands, similarly to Kant's *Metaphysical Elements of Justice*, within the scholastic tradition characterized by the combination of the doctrines of law and ethics. It is thus in the first place political theory in the general sense in which Aristotle had understood ethics as a "political science" (ἐπιστήμη πολιτική), insofar as for it, ethical action has its place in the "polis" (in "society"), while the political order, for its part, has its foundation and its reason for being located in the ethical realization of freedom. Then there is the respect in which, for Hegel, the *Philosophy of Right* has its decisive contemporary political significance: it takes up and resolves the problem of "dichotomy," which has come to be the condition of contemporary existence at all levels with the emergence of modern society and its political revolution. However, Hegel's coming to grips with this problem of the age, grounded in the social and political upheaval, is in no way limited to the *Philosophy of Right* and to those writings of his, such as *Natural Law: The Scientific Ways of Treating Natural Law: Its Place in Moral Philosophy, and Its Relation to the Positive Sciences of Law* (1802), in which there is a directly recognizable connection with questions of political order; this is rather constitutive for his philosophy in its entirety, inasmuch as it is the philosophy of reason and of being in relation to its age, as that age is historically determined by the dichotomy. Therefore, in virtually all of Hegel's writings and lectures from his Jena publications on, and already in the youthful writings of the Bern and Frankfurt periods, one finds considerations of the Revolution and its philosophy, as well as considerations of the romantic-restorative philosophy of subjectivity and its flight from political-historical reality; and this frequently occurs—as in the *Phenomenology*, the *Philosophy of History*, and the *History of Philosophy*—at the focal points of the argument, where decisions of principle find expression. It is certainly possible to understand religion, art, right, world history, and philosophy as spheres of life which Hegel turned to one after another in their givenness. Then, however, the deeper philosophical connection does not get expressed. According to the theories of emancipation, world history should come to its end with the modern world; for the philosophy of subjectivity, aesthetic art becomes the power of the poetic overcoming of dichotomy and the bearer of the reestablishment of the "old world" destroyed by the Enlightenment and revolution. A theology of pure inwardness is at hand limiting religion to feeling and abandoning social and political reality to the atheism of the understanding. Thus, with Hegel, it is everywhere a matter of confronting the problem of the age that has been posed by the political and social revolution. For him, it is the point of reference around which the threads of philosophical thought are connected into the whole of the system. Therefore this thought nowhere steps entirely out of the political context. At the same time, it thus also always comprises the presupposition for Hegel's immediate and explicit confrontation with the political problems of the age, in his political essays as well.

The bibliography cannot do justice to this universal significance of the political for Hegel's philosophy; it must restrict itself to the works which have state and society thematically as their object. Because of this, it runs the danger of fostering the idea that the political problem has solely a limited, as it were "special" significance for Hegel and that the only works important for its understanding are those that directly address it. Dilthey understood Hegel's development in his youth essentially from the standpoint of religion; Lukàcs interpreted it purely politically. His work therefore belongs simply in virtue of its problematic within the scope of the bibliography, whereas Dilthey's presentation must remain outside it. Nevertheless, the formulation of political questions by the young Hegel is only properly understood by those who also see the religious context pointed out by Dilthey, which first makes comprehensible in general the passionate partisanship which Hegel's concern with the revolution then signified. This is just one example among many. There are treatments that, without touching upon the political problems, still deal with these decisively important relationships in his philosophy; and on the other hand, there are works on Hegel's philosophy of law, state, and history which understand his concepts so formally and so exclusively within the context of the system that the connection of Hegel's philosophy with the political problems of his age and its current political significance disappear. The material difficulty lying here for the bibliography cannot be removed; it must suffice to make reference to it and take notice of the one-sidedness which cannot be avoided.

The central significance of the political problem for Hegel's philosophy has had the result that, above all in the period from 1830 to 1848, and then up until today, the more important treatments of it have been made not in the realm of scientific philosophy, but in political ideologies, as well as in the political writing of history and in political and legal theories. The relation of Marx and Engels to Hegel, which stands today so much in the foreground, is only one example of the degree to which the consideration of Hegel's philosophy has become a continually influential component of the history of political ideas up until the present. Both the right and left have claimed it for themselves, but even within political groups and tendencies there are passionate positions for and against it. Whereas, for example, Rosenkranz and Sietze celebrate Hegelian philosophy as the incarnation of the Prussian spirit, K. E. Schubarth condemns Hegel's philosophy of state as "incompatible with the highest principle of life and development of the Prussian state." For this reason, Varnhagen von Ense writes at that time: "We thus wish to corroborate our observation that the Hegelian philosophy of state, for a long time besmirched for its servility, but recently condemned for its liberalism, its concealed call to revolt, has by now fortunately run through every type of suspicion which no superior work can escape" (both quotations are cited following Hoffmeister's notes, *Hegels Briefe*, vol. III, p. 407 ff.).

This cycle of awe and condemnation remains typical of the

controversy-ridden history of Hegel's political influence up to this very day. Whereas after 1945, he became the father and originator of fascism for Popper, v. Martin, and others, Hegel's philosophy never played a role similar to that of Nietzsche for Nazism. Nevertheless, even there, controversy persisted when Hegel was considered. Whereas for Steding (*Das Reich und die Krankheit der europaischen Kultur*, Hamburg 1938, 1942) he is the true prophet of the "Third Reich," others rejected him as a philosopher of European universality and thus as an opponent of the national renewal "bound to the German people."

This grappling with Hegel, continuing since his own day in a push and shove of advocacy and rejection, does not come to rest in Hegel scholarship. Here as well the conception of his philosophy is not yet fixed; his thought has not been definitively integrated into the history of culture either politically-historically or philosophically; the problems which animate it are still (or again) problems of contemporary life. Thus historical and philosophical research has also come to be infused with the positive and critical standpoints of encounter with and attachment to Hegel; open or concealed, there is still a tendency to understand Hegel in the context of contemporary problems and thus to make his philosophy an element in the determination of one's own path by either appropriating or rejecting it. Whereas one important school, following from Dilthey, has understood Hegel's philosophy primarily from its origins in the theological-religious, "irrational" problematic of his Bern and Frankfurt period, and have thus taken it out of its political-historical context, the frequent interpretation of his political theory up to this day has remained bound to the examination of the relation of state, nation, and people and the problem of the totalitarian state. The social problem, on the contrary, at first retreated entirely into the background, especially in Germany; the significant line of influence leading from Hegel to Lorenz v. Stein broke off. It was the confrontation with Marxism that first led here to a change; Hegel's philosophy of society was approached anew from the standpoint of the development leading from it by way of the Young Hegelians to Marx, but then in its own right as well. In the meantime, it has become the object of striking investigations not only in France, but also in England and the United States.

The bibliographies on Hegel's political philosophy, provided by K. Gründer in a first German edition (1956) covering the years 1905–1956 and in a second German edition (1965) containing a selected bibliography for the years 1821–1965, and by H. M. Sass in a French edition (1969) covering the years 1821–1903, all stand under the conditions of these difficulties.

II

The idea of the possibility of going to Berlin first came up in Hegel's correspondence in a letter to Paulus written on July 30, 1814 from Nurnberg. His wish to return again to the university was "unconquerable." Certainly "for several years" there existed prospects for an appointment at Erlangen; nevertheless, under the "present conditions" he had to pursue another opportunity (Br. 235). Hoffmeister refers to this letter in his note 3 (vol. II, p. 376), stating that the professors there had fallen into poverty due to a year-long delay of salary (concerning the general situation at Erlangen University see Br. 223, note 1, vol. II, p. 372). Hegel had now learned that Fichte's chair (Fichte died on January 29, 1814) was still unoccupied; Paulus might therefore attempt to find out more about the plans there and "make mention" of Hegel (see also Br. 236 and 241). The letter to Niethammer of October 26, 1824 refers as well to the Berlin possibilities: "Abroad" one knows better "what one wants, including universities and learning" (Br. 243). However, Hegel also just as much looks towards Jena, where Schelling, settled in Munich, had refused a position (Br. 262), and towards Heidelberg, in so far as Fries is "engaged" there (Br. 263). In all these considerations the question of income plays no small role; thus Hegel writes to Frommann on April 14, 1816 concerning Jena that he could not go there "with the usual philosophy professor's pay," although he "had the impression that prospects could open up in Jena" (Br. 262). Concerning the details of the events preceding Hegel's call to Berlin, see what Hoffmeister relates in note 1 to Br 278 (to v. Raumer), vol. II, pp. 397–403.

All in all, the letters reveal that what stood in that foreground for Hegel concerning appointments to a university, and thus also concerning the appointment at Berlin, were the usual and thoroughly typical considerations, such as the possibilities of effectiveness and research, the relations in the departments, questions of salary, and so forth. The decision to go to Berlin was also in the first instance a matter of his university career; nowhere in his correspondence does one find statements which suggest that Hegel proceeded in his considerations from some internal connection between his philosophy and Prussia and Prussian policy. What Berlin offered was the better endowment of a philosophy professorship, and then, most importantly, the further positive arrangement extended to Hegel and his philosophy by the "philosophizing minister" (Boisserée, see Hoffmeister note 1 to Br. 326, vol. II, p. 422), Baron von Altenstein, who led the newly created Prussian "Ministry for Cultural, Educational and Medical Affairs" since November 3, 1817 (see Br. 326, 328, 331, 332, 333, 337, 338, 339, 341, 343). Although Hegel, simply as a Schwabian, prefers southern Germany, Berlin is the freer city, more favorable to philosophy, philosophical influence, and scholarly education. That tips the balance. "You know," writes Hegel on June 9, 1821 from Berlin to Niethammer (Br. 390), "that I have come here in order to be in a center of things and not in a province." Hegel's Estates Assembly essay of 1817 shows sufficiently how he judged the state of affairs in southern Germany, particularly in Wurtemberg, and the political "nullity" and "deadness" reigning there (see *Hegel's Political Writings*, pp. 252f.). This turning away from the provinces is certainly political in motive in the form it takes with Hegel. It has to do with his deep aversion to the restorative tendencies tied to the provincial narrowness and thus stands in direct contradiction to the intentions which according to Haym are supposed to have influenced Hegel's decision to go to Berlin. The correspondence itself unambiguously shows that the identification of Hegel with "Prussian reaction" has nothing to do with the real course of things. It belongs to the period after 1830 in the struggle against the then actually reactionary policy of Prussia, and thus it rests upon the subsequent, politically conditioned identification of Hegelian philosophy with this reaction. The first biography of Hegel, written by K. Rosenkranz (*G. W. F. Hegels Leben*, Berlin 1844), admittedly from entirely different motives—R. wrote an "Apologia" for Hegel versus Haym in 1858—also played a not unessential role in the emergence of the idea that Hegel's philosophy was an essentially Prussian philosophy. In this work Rosenkranz attempted, through a supposed application of Hegel's speculative method to his biography, to "deduce" Hegel's Berlin teaching activity from an inner correspondence between the world spirit at work in Prussia and that teaching through Hegel. Prussia, an artificial state, protected by no natural borders and not yet consolidated, was urged to "maintain its position" solely "through the restless progress of its cultural development." Therein lay in the first instance the significance of Kant, who gave the Prussian "the philosophy corresponding to him." However, for Hegel to have consummated Kantian philosophy, his philosophy must also stand as the consummation of Prussian philosophy. So it is lit-

erally stated: "Now that Hegelian philosophy is in truth the consummation of Kantian philosophy, there thus arises the higher
necessity which brought about Hegel's appointment in Prussia
and the quick taking-root there of his philosophy" (317). This
"higher necessity" has thus brought about his appointment:
"What many regarded merely as the satisfaction of a life-long
wish of minister Altenstein was actually the work of the progressive tendency of the Prussian spirit" (316ff.). A particularly
crass example of the "application" of Hegel's speculative method
to Prussia is provided by Karl Friedrich F. Sietze, *Grundbegriff
Preussischer Staats- und Rechtsgeschichte*, Berlin 1829. Sietze here
deduces Prussian history with Hegelian concepts and analogizes
it with Christian dogmatics, relating The Lord's Prayer, the trin-
itarian doxology, to Austria, Prussia, and the Slavs (particularly
p. xvi, 430, 442, 480, 643–650). The German Empire is the consciousness of Europe (643, 650), whereas Prussia is its self-consciousness (671), the revelation (698), and the body of the Lord
(699). The book appeared during the lifetime of Hegel, the
"greatly honored teacher" (481). No statement by Hegel concerning it is known of; a letter of December 14, 1830 to Spietze
merely alludes to his relation to Hamann and to his "comic
streak" (Br. 660). The idea of an inner connection between Hegel's philosophy and Prussia rests upon such "deductions"; it is
evidently not easy even for historical sense to free itself of intu-
itions that are fixed upon by a political and ideological interest.

It is the great merit of E. Weil's outstanding study of Hegel's
philosophy of state (*Hegel et l'Etat*, Paris 1950) to have demonstrated in detail how little justified it is to equate the Prussia in
which Hegel lived in 1818 with the then truly reactionary Prussia of the eighteen thirties and forties. In the Napoleonic Wars,
absolutist Prussia was destroyed; in its reconstruction, the government recognized that only a radical reform would be in a
position to strengthen the power of the state. Thus the worst

restrictions on freedom were done away with, the sale of landed property was decontrolled, villeinage was abolished, the greatest part of the noble's privileges was removed, and the peasants were freed, while the towns obtained an autonomous administration (18f.). E. Weil sums up his account by concluding that Prussia was at that time a progressive state ("an advanced state," 19) in comparison to the France of the restoration or to England before the reforms of 1832 and to Metternich's Austria. Here lie the presuppositions for the positive relation which Hegel then had to the Prussian state, not in the reactionary tendencies that also manifest themselves there, and thus also not in the notion that Prussia was for him the incorporation of the absolute state power annihilating the modern principles of freedom and rational law: "In 1830 as in 1818, Hegel therefore considers Prussia to be the modern state par excellence (which seems to be exactly the viewpoint of the historian), and regards it thus because he sees it founded upon liberty" (22). For Hegel, this progressive character of Prussia comes into force especially at Berlin University, and the inaugural address which he there delivered on October 22, 1818 (*Berliner Schriften*, pp. 3–21) perhaps best illustrates the ideas and expectations with which he came to Berlin in order "at this juncture" and "from the local point of view, to enter upon a broader academic influence." The "misery of the age" is now over; for a long time the "high interests of reality" had to stand in the foreground in the struggles "to reestablish and save the political totality of the life of the people and of the state," and "drawing to themselves all powers of the spirit, and the forces of all classes." Now, however, the time has come for "the free realm of thought to blossom independently within the state" (3f.). Everything "that should be valid" must from now on "justify" itself "before insight and thought." Prussia, however, has created space for this free effectiveness of spirit in a particular way: "Here, the formation and the flowering of the sciences is one of the essential elements, even in the life of the state." This opens the prospect that philosophy at Berlin University, the "university of the hub" of the nation, will find its "place and preeminent cultivation" (4).

Hegel understood his influence in Berlin and its connection with the Prussian state in this manner. The relation in which his philosophy stands to politics in general becomes visible. His philosophy cuts through the foreground of the political struggle of the day and its formalism, and conceives the free spiritual activity of the person and his genuine personal life within the civil order as the substantial end whose realization is ultimately what the free state is about. Hegel's correspondence in these Berlin years shows how his own life had its center in his post and in "family contentment" (see Br. 355) and so stood in a beautiful and peaceful harmony with the philosophical thought of personal freedom.

III

E. Weil (p. 11) points out that even a series of good studies from the last thirty years have not been able to prevent a further stubborn persistence of the picture of Hegel's philosophy coined by the political critique of Hegel in the nineteenth century: "Just as Plato is the inventor of ideas, . . . Aristotle is the man of formal logic, . . . Descartes the hero of clarity, and Kant the champion of rigor, Hegel is the man for whom the state is all, the individual is nothing, and morality is a subordinate form of the life of spirit: in a word he is the apologist of the Prussian state." That gets confirmed ever again. So, according to Hook (p. 19, n. 1), Haym judged too mildly: "the situation stands even worse for Hegel than it was pictured by the most critical of his biographers." His idealism is the justification of the existing order through the ambiguous formulation of the identity of reason and reality (18). Everything, however, that has ever been said against Hegel as a "reactionary" and against his deification of the state is surpassed by K. Popper, *The Open Society and its Enemies* (vol. II, The High Tide of Prophecy: Hegel and Marx), London first 1945, 2nd ed. (revised) 1952 (II, c. 12, Hegel and the New Tribalism, pp. 27–80). The age of dishonesty and irresponsibility begins in Germany with German Idealism; Hegel was employed by the reactionary faction of Prussia in order to serve their demands (29). He did this, insofar as he renewed the philosophy of Heraclitus, Plato, and Aristotle, the first enemies of the "open society" (30). Since then Hegelianism has reigned in Germany: "Hegelianism is the renaissance of tribalism" (30), such that, for Popper, Hegel's philosophy is nothing other than the link between Platonic and modern fascism (31). However, its radical collectivism derives not only from Plato, but also just as much from Friedrich Wilhelm III: what is common to both is the message that the state is everything and the individual is nothing (31). In this regard, Hegel not once showed any talent (32), and thus his philosophy shows "how easily a clown may be a 'maker of history'" (32). According to Popper, the proposition of the identity of the rational and the real results in the doctrine "that might is right" (41), into which Hegel had perverted the ideas of 1789 by replacing humanity with totalitarian nationalism (49) and with Prussian authoritarianism (56, 58, and passim) and so forth. . . . In "Hegel: Legende und Wirklichkeit" (first in English in *The Philos. Review* IX, no. 4, Oct. 1951, then in German in the *Z. f. Philos. Forschung* X, no. 2, 1956, pp. 191–226), W. Kaufman has now taken a stand towards this curious book in which Popper resurrects not only Haym's critique, but Schopenhauer's litanies of hatred against Hegel; what must objectively be said to Popper is masterfully presented in this essay. It concludes with the demand that "Hegel finally be done justice" "now that Hegelianism and Antihegelianism have had their day" (226). Following the first world war, V. Basch (*Les Doctrines politiques des philosophes classiques de l'Allemagne*, Paris 1927) already defended Hegel against certain tendencies to interpret his philosophy purely in terms of the nation-state, and against the charge of "pan-Germanism." In an essay entitled "Politik und Moral in Hegels Philosophie" (*Bl. f. d. Philos.* VIII, 1934, pp. 127ff.), H. Heimsoeth has particularly pointed out the positive significance of the freedom of the individual and, on this basis, corrected the one-sided interpretation of the principle of power (*ibid.*, pp. 143ff.). In this context, besides Weil, Marcuse must especially be mentioned. According to him, the emergence of fascism makes necessary a new interpretation of Hegelian philosophy. One finds "that Hegel's basic concepts are hostile to the tendencies that have led into fascist theory and practice" (Marcuse preface, p. vii). Hegel's problem was the anarchic aspect in the social and economic development of civil society (60). Certainly his philosophy thus also contains an immanent critique of liberalist society, but he aims at making clear that in it tendencies are at work which lead necessarily to the authoritarian state (59, see 178f.). Thus Hegel's philosophy is determined by the intention to counter this danger. Vaughan's treatment (*Studies in the History of Political Thought*) is distinguished by its independence from the usual prejudices. He interprets Hegel's political philosophy with regard to the history of protest against its "abstract treatment" in the eighteenth century. His special achievement lies in combining the "historical sense of Vico with the philosophical genius of Kant and Fichte" (143). His philosophy thus succeeds in establishing the inner unity of reason and history and thereby tearing down the abstract barrier which up till then had separated the ethical existence of man from his political growth. The stubbornness with which the image of Hegel created by his political opponents in the middle of the preceding century nevertheless persists is also based upon the fact that, after the so-called collapse of German Idealism and up through our own day, academic philosophy and its histories of philosophy have lost almost all contact with the problems of civil society. Its treatment became a matter for sociology, pursued as a specialized science, and possibly for cultural history, such that even in Dilthey's *Jugendgeschichte Hegels* (1905), which has had such decisive significance for the renewal of Hegel research in German, Hegel's political theory is mentioned either not at all or only in passing.

So it has happened that in the second half of the nineteenth century, besides Lorenz von Stein (see P. Vogel, *Hegels Gesellschaftsbegriff*, Berlin 1925, pp. 125–207), only Marx and Engels knew of the epochal significance of Hegelian philosophy and held fast to the problems it addressed. For them as well, Hegel's philosophy, as philosophy, is "reactionary" and an "expression of the old world" (Marx: "This metaphysics is the metaphysical expression of the old world as truth of the new worldview," cited following Rjazanov, MEGA I, 1, p. xxxv).

It is this, however, not because it stands in the service of Prussian reaction, but rather because it is an attempt to overcome spiritually and speculatively the revolution occurring with the emergence of civil society, the revolution which it, on the other hand, was the only philosophy at all to have understood in its essence and universal significance. Therefore they both turned passionately against the liberal critique of Hegel and its identification of Hegel with Prussia, calling it a "disgrace to want to dismiss a fellow like Hegel as a Prussian" (see the remarks from a letter of May 1860 cited by Weil, pp. 15f.). In 1888, at a time when Hegel was otherwise almost entirely forgotten and had no influence any longer, Fr. Engels still referred to him as a "creative genius," pointed to the "innumerable treasures" contained in the "immense building" of the system, and defended it against Hegel's "pygmy opponents" and their "terrible fuss"

Appendix to Hegel and the French Revolution

(*Ludwig Feuerbach and the End of Classical German Philosophy*, in Marx and Engels, *Basic Writings on Politics and Philosophy*, Doubleday, New York, 1959, p. 202). In a letter to Friedrich Albert Lange on March 29, 1865, Engels also writes in a similar vein: "I am naturally no longer a Hegelian, but I still have a great reverence and devotion to the old colossal fellow" (printed in the *Neue Zeit*, vol. 28, no. I [1910], pp. 183–186, cited following Karl Vorländer: *Kant, Fichte, Hegel und der Sozialismus*, Berlin 1920, pp. 26–27). So the paradoxical situation has arisen, in which the new uncovering of the greatest political philosophy that modern civil society has produced as its own philosophy, today issues and must issue from those who have become its world-historical opponents.

IV

After 1830, the critique of Hegel generally serves the task of emancipation from metaphysics and its tradition. This holds not only for the Left Hegelians. F. J. Stahl (*Die Philosophie des Rechts, I. Gesch, d. Rechtsphilos.*, 1847) is also "keenly convinced" of the "untruth" of Hegel's philosophy. For him, this untruth is philosophy with its dialectical method; it leads necessarily to the "pantheistic system" and thereby brings Hegel into opposition to Christianity and its personified God, and annihilates "personhood and freedom" (453) and "true reality" (450) as well. That is in principle the same argument Haym employs: philosophy as such leads away from reality and puts a "dream world" in its place. Therefore Hegel must first of all "surreptitiously obtain" a reality; and he thereby loses all connection with historical reality (467) and the principles ruling it. Thus it is necessary, on the one hand, to fight against his "philosophical system as an absolute and pernicious false doctrine," while, however, on the other hand, preserving the positive achievements that Hegel accomplished; namely, his doctrine of the power of ethical life, his overcoming of the civil-law political theory of v. Haller (467, see in this regard Rosenzweig II, 191f.), the fruitful approaches to an historical view, etc., so that one makes his theory "fully independent of his system" (465). In the case of Stahl, this detaching of Hegel's political-historical theories from his philosophy leads to its alteration and actual destruction as much as does its "leftist" reinterpretation as a reactionary ideology. This critique of Hegel had further influence. Thus Plenge (*Marx und Hegel*, Tübingen 1911, p. 45) states that the "constructions of Hegelian metaphysics cover over the brilliant colors of this great picture like a dull varnish"; the metaphysics has as its immediate consequence that Hegel must remain "blind" to the "creative possibilities of the nineteenth century" (52). For Spengler (*Preussentum und Sozialismus*, 1920, p. 79), Hegel is a political thinker with so strong a sense of reality that recent philosophy can boast of no one his equal, "if one sets aside Hegel's metaphysics" (see Giese's critique of this in *Hegels Staatsidee und der Begriff der Staatserziehung*, Halle 1926, p. 9 and p. 9 n. 3). An analogous process plays itself out in the critical dismissal of the historical science of Hegel. Here as well philosophy becomes mere speculation in its relation to history, such that the cultivation of historical method coincides with philosophy's destruction. For Zeller (*Die Philos. d. Griechen in ihrer gesch. Entwicklung dargestellt*, 1859–1868, Tübingen/Leipzig 1923, I, introduction, p. 10ff.) Hegel's history of the Idea turns into the history of ideas which men have made for themselves; thereby the Idea gets destroyed as the principle of history and the history of philosophy gets detached from the presupposition of philosophy itself. The one-sidedness of the philosophical sublation of philosophy's political content belongs to the one-sidedness of the political sublation of philosophy. Both forms of the sublation led in the nineteenth century to Hegel's historization.

V

The notion of philosophy as theory of its age corresponds in the *Philosophy of Right* to the attention paid to the history of the day insofar as current events are the political reality in which philosophy has to conceive presently existing reason. Therefore the political-publicistic works of Hegel belong in a direct sense to his philosophy, just as the newspaper and its reading always played an important role for him: "The morning reading of the newspaper is a kind of realistic morning prayer. One orients one's attitude toward the world with respect to God or with respect to what the world is. The latter provides the same security as prayer, in that one knows where one stands." (*Aphorismen der Jenenser Zeit* no. 31, Dok. 360). W. R. Beyer (*Zwischen Phänomenologie und Logik, Hegel als Redakteur der Bamberger Zeitung*, Frankfurt/ Main 1955) points out Hegel's constant "wish for periodicals" and bases it upon the fact that for him, it was a matter of "transforming actual events into theory by means of the periodical" (39). Beyer therefore argues against viewing Hegel's Bamberg editorial activity mainly as a meaningless episode with no relation to his philosophy (see in this regard the [preceding] note 11), and presents in his discussion new material on the situation in Bamberg and Hegel's effectiveness there which is important for understanding his political philosophy and his political ideas in general. Thus Beyer justifiably stresses the philosophical significance of publicist activity for Hegel; but, on the other hand, he ascribes a function to Hegel's publicist activity in relation to his philosophy which it first acquires for his critics. Hegel was the first—at least in Germany—to comprehend that the political and social revolution occurring in France and England drags into its torrent of change the entire human condition in all its spheres; and therefore he raised philosophy to the theory of the age, directing it to penetrate political events and critically address the ideologies within them. Here one has the reason why both the liberal and revolutionary opposition to the existing order understood themselves in their critical encounter with Hegel as a "realization of philosophy" (in this regard, see Horst Stuke, *August Cieszkowski und Bruno Bauer. Studie zum Problem der "Verwirklichung der Philosophie" bei den Junghegelianern.* [phil. diss. Münster 1957; reworked and published as *Philosophie der Tat*, Stuttgart 1963], particularly concerning the significance of this encounter for the unfolding of Marxist political theory), and why then the transformation of philosophy into political publicist activity, and the philosopher into the publicist, is also entailed in this realization (see in this regard Beyer, p. 39ff. and passim). Beyer's thesis that philosophy needs the press in order to have influence and be realized (71ff.) thus precisely touches upon the relationship in which philosophy and press stand to one another for the political opposition and especially for the Young Hegelians in the years up until 1848. However, for them it also entails at the same time the destruction of philosophy, that is, of Hegelian philosophy; and thus in their case, the relation of philosophy and publicist activity is the reverse of what it is for Hegel. Whereas for Hegel, philosophy conceives the truth of the age, for the Young Hegelians, the age demands the sublation of the truth of philosophy. This decisive difference gets slighted in Beyer's treatment of Hegel's publicist activity. Because for him the theory of Marx is essentially a continuation and further development of Hegelian thought (see 230), the positive meaning of Hegel's political theory comes out both more directly and more clearly for him in the publicist activity of Hegel concerned with the "realization of philosophy" than in his philosophy, which rather has the function of obscuring it and making possible the avoidance of its consequences. The theoretical labor which, as philosophy, is for Marx the "preparatory work for subsequent action and also for an action by others, the masses" (75), is for Hegel the object itself, in the form of the concept of those grounds in the happenings of the age which make their appearance for that age in political practice and ideology, but neither on the side of revolution nor on the side of restoration. The progression from Hegel to Marx therefore simultaneously entails, as a progression, the destruction of philosophy and thus the break with Hegel. Beyer sees this also (see his critical comments on the attempts "wanting unconditionally to save Hegel for Marx" [97f.]); but as for what is destroyed in this break, for him it is the retrograde character of Hegelian theory, consisting in the philosophy itself, which he regards as the limit upon its "implicitly" progressive content. Hegel himself always saw his true goal to lie in philosophy and academic teaching, not only during his Bamberg activity, but also in his school post in Nurmberg; this is fully confirmed by his correspondence in these years. Thus Hegel complains (in a letter from Bamberg to Knebel), "of being hindered by so-called fate from producing something through labor that would be more able to satisfy men of insight and taste in my science—and that could provide me with the satisfaction of being able to say: for this have I lived!" (Br. 109). His thoughts are constantly occupied with university issues, and not only in regard to his own career possibilities (see for example, Br. 122). In Bamberg, the main thing is not the newspaper, but the work on his *Logic* which "now begins to take shape" (Br. 122 of May 20, 1808 to Niethammer). Corresponding to this, he viewed his editorial activity from the start as an "engagement" which he enters into "temporarily . . . for two, three years" (Br. 98 of May 30, 1807 to Niethammer), although it has the advantages of "still leaving time for my scientific work to survive" (*ibid.*). The newspaper cannot be regarded as "a solid establishment," "as tempting as the isolated independence is," because the work of a "newspaper writer," although certainly "something public," is nevertheless "frankly not a position" (*ibid.*). Thus, although the connection with publicist activity, whose significance has first really been elaborated upon by Beyer's book, remains so important for Hegel's philosophy, the Bamberg activity is, no differently than the Nurmberg school post, still only an interim waystation towards the true vocation of holding an academic teaching position.

VI

For the development of Hegel's political philosophy in his Tübingen, Bern, and Frankfurt period, Rosenzweig's *Hegel und der Staat*, Munich 1920, vol. I (see especially pp. 17ff., 33ff., 77ff.) is still indispensable; this applies as well to the important chapters which cover the Jena period (pp. 101ff.).

In the general treatments of Hegel's intellectual development, the constitutive significance of the French Revolution and coming to grips with it politically for Hegelian philosophy and its development recedes almost completely into the background under the influence of Dilthey and his work—pathbreaking for the renewal of Hegel studies—*Jugendgeschichte Hegels* (1905, *Ges. Schr.* IV); this holds also for Haering (Hegel, *Sein Wollen und sein Werk*, vol. I, 1929), Justus Schwarz (*Hegels geistige Entwicklung*, Frankfurt/Main 1938), and Glockner, among others. Glockner, in his biography (*Hegel*, two volumes, Stuttgart 1929 and 1940), does deal with Hegel's relation to the French Revolution and to the day-to-day life of politics, and observes that his "sense for political affairs" was always "very strongly developed" (see I, 385 ff.), only to then exclude the analysis of Hegel's political essays "insofar as the details are not important from a humane or philosophical point of view" (387 n. 1). Later on he writes that also Hegel's "legal and political theory" has "nothing to do with his political publicist activity" because the former are "not at all occasional writings" but "belong to his system" (I, 393 n. 1). In this manner, the political element is excluded from his philosophy: the latter's systematic problems grow out of relationships which have no essential significance for the political events of the time.

In dealing with this depolitization of Hegelian philosophy, Lukács has demonstrated, following Marx, that Hegel's development is decisively determined from the beginning by his encounter not only with the French Revolution, but also, from the time of his Bern period on, with the Industrial Revolution in England. Hegel is the "only philosopher of the period following Kant to make a truly original approach to the problems of the age"; an analysis of the writings of his youth shows "how all the problems of dialectics grew out of his reflections on the two great world-historical facts of the age: the French Revolution and the Industrial Revolution in England" (*The Young Hegel*, translated by Rodney Livingstone, Merlin Press, London 1975, pp. 565, 566). However, because for Lukács the positive content of Hegelian dialectics is first set free through its subordination to political-revolutionary practice and thus through the destruction of its philosophical-metaphysical form by Marx, the positive thesis of this book is at the same time developed as an antithesis to the idealistic and religious, cultural-historical interpretation of the young Hegel. Just as the political problem disappears for the latter, so all content of Hegelian thought which cannot be traced back to political and social problems loses its independent significance for Lukács. The acceptance of a " 'theological' period" of Hegel is a "reactionary legend" (*ibid.*, p. 3); his thought certainly develops itself in the form of religious and metaphysical notions, through which, however, its real content is shrouded in "a mystical fog" (*ibid.*, 82) and twisted into something idealistic. (The religious and theological content of Hegel's philosophy is developed in a positive manner, in direct connection with his concept of reason, by Johannes Flügge in *Die sittlichen Grundla-*

gen des Denkens. Hegels existentielle Erkenntnisgesinnung, Hamburg 1953.) Nevertheless, the great service of this book is indisputable (see Hermann Lübbe, *Zur marxistische Auslegung Hegels*, Philos. Rundschau 2, 1954/5, pp. 38–60 [on Lukács and Bloch]). It goes beyond the preceding immanent theological and philosophical portrayals of Hegel's development during his youth, and makes it necessary to raise the questions of what it means for Hegel's philosophy that it unfolded in a consideration of the problems of political-social reality, and what it means for the latter that their resolution according to Hegel required philosophy and its speculative concept.

Regarding literature on the relation of Marx and Hegel see the bibliographies referred to in sec. I of this Appendix.

VII

Hegel's philosophy of world history is the developed theory of historicity, which for him is constitutive for all concepts of man's being and for philosophy itself. "Geist" is, as Marcuse observes, the concept which designates reason in its historicity: "The term that designates reason as history is mind (Geist), which denotes the historical world viewed in relation to the rational progress of humanity" (Marcuse, *op. cit.*, 10f. See also in this regard H. Marcuse's earlier work: *Hegels Ontologie und die Grundlegung einer Theorie der Geschichtlichkeit*, Frankfurt/Main 1932). Although Hegel can therefore designate the substance that makes history into world-history both as "spirit" and "Reason" (see, for example, the *Philosophy of History*, pp. 9f.), he can supplant both with freedom, because freedom is the historical realization of spirit and thus is reason as it is directed to this realization (see pp. 17f.). All these concepts thus have nothing to do with "Idealism" and an idealistic "spiritualization" of real history, but rather have the task of establishing history as the reality from whose process the determination of man, reason, and freedom cannot be disengaged. Thereby they belong directly in the context of Hegel's consideration of the abstract, anti-historical theory of reason and freedom advanced by the Enlightenment and the French Revolution. Historicity is asserted against this abstractness. For Enlightenment philosophy up through Comte's consummation of its concept, history is also the "world history of humanity"; to that extent one can generally say that Hegel's philosophy of history arises from it and presupposes it. However, whereas for Enlightenment philosophy and its positivist successors the present (in accord with the principle of progress, that the later is the better) completes preceding history by freeing men from it, Hegel's philosophy of world history serves to demonstrate that the present is the completion of preceding world history, not because it annuls its substantial content, but because it brings it to a universal realization.

Concerning the development of Hegel's theory of world history, reference can be made to Rosenzweig (II, 178ff.), Busse (*Hegels Phänomenologie des Geistes und der Staat*, Berlin 1931, pp. 120ff.), and Marcuse (pp. 224ff.); regarding its precedents in German Idealism, see H. Lübbe (*Die Transzendentalphilosophie und das Problem der Geschichte. Untersuchungen zur Genesis der Geschichtsphilosophie* [Kant, Fichte and Schelling], Habil. Schr. Erlangen 1957.

VIII

It is generally not sufficiently noticed that Hegel's deep distaste for student fraternities and demagogic intrigues (Br. 358, 359) essentially springs from the same presuppositions as his negative attitude towards the restorative trends in Germany. Both movements reflect the narrowness of the German state of affairs and their lack of all relation to the real historical-political tasks of the age, the political "nullity" whose reign in the "much praised land of German-dumb" (Br. 241) Hegel knew how to mock so bitterly. Rosenzweig (II, 206) has pointed out that for Hegel liberal and conservative Romanticism belong together in their "hatred of the law." Not freedom as such, but the political activity that means to stand at its service, is for Hegel what is objectionable as the "shallow thinking" which foregoes every type of thoroughgoing knowledge and instead claims that only that "is true which each individual allows to rise out of his heart, emotion, and inspiration about . . . the state, the government, and the constitution" (*Philosophy of Right*, Preface, pp. 6,5). Hegel recognized in these movements, as perhaps only Goethe also did, the profound danger of the anarchic element which threatens everywhere where mere subjectivity and its feeling are made the standard of political orders. That is the meaning of the notoriously famous phrase, "the broth of heart." The harm is that the student fraternities, and their philosophical leader Fries with them, take "the rich inward articulation of ethical life, i.e. the state, the architectonic of that life's rationality which . . . uses the strict accuracy of measurement which holds together every pillar, arch, and buttress and thereby produces the strength of the whole out of the harmony of the parts—and confound the completed fabric in the broth of 'heart, friendship, and inspiration'" (6). Where thus "subjective feeling" and the "particular conviction" are to decide all, there principles are at work from which "follows the ruin of the inner ethical life and a good conscience, of love and right dealing between private persons, no less than the ruin of public order and the law of the land" (8). Therefore Hegel also speaks of "bubbling over" and "fanaticism" (for example, in Br. 356), etc., to describe the uncultivated youthfulness and fundamentally pseudo-political character of these movements and strivings (in this regard, see also Marcuse pp. 180f., who points to the pseudo-democratic character of these movements).

Hegel nevertheless personally interceded in many cases with testimony and petitions on behalf of suspects and accused, such as Asverus (see Br. 358), de Wette (Br. 359, as well as n. 10, vol. II, pp. 446f.), Carové (Br. 377), and Cousin in connection with his unfortunate Dresden arrest (Br. 486); and he did not break off relations with them so far as they were in any way personally connected with him. (See in this regard the rich documentary material which Hoffmeister has collected in the above-mentioned letters and presented in his notes.)

Hegel understood the censorship and police measures, which he found equally intolerable, as essentially a reaction to the activity of the student fraternities, just as the act of Sand had certainly directly provoked them; he did not unduly burden the Prussian state with these "political censorship regulations," especially since they were "to some extent common to the whole federation" (see Br. 359). However, as Hegel writes in the same letter to Creuzer, the public pitch is not raised by all these notes, and the days are accompanied by hope and fear. He himself endures the "demagogic misery with peril" and hopes to remain undisturbed by it henceforth as well (Br. 390). He holds himself back and lives "on the periphery or rather outside it without any relation to the active and causative sphere" (Br. 355), and openly admits his anxiety to his friend Niethammer, which makes it conprehensible why it "doesn't exactly suit him to see a storm rise up every year" (Br. 390).

In a retrospective glance at philosophy and the critique of philosophy in the years 1833–1838, A. Ruge has attempted to characterize Hegel's attitude (*Aus früherer Zeit*, vol. IV, Berlin 1867, pp. 549ff.). To begin with, Ruge affirms that Hegel has presented the "most profound concept of the state that humanity has yet achieved." He has "read the Greeks with too much reason, and lived through his age, the age of revolution, with too clear an awareness, not to have gone beyond the "family state" and the state of civil society, and to arrive at the dictate that the state be in the form of a public, self-determining entity" (551). However, one can rightly condemn Hegel for later letting his position count only theoretically and not denouncing the political "nullity" of the state of affairs of German government, of which he was as clearly aware as others. Considering the then existing necessity of practical opposition, it was an injustice for him to have rebuked the idealists and demagogues for their "mere imperative and demands" (557). Ruge calls Hegel's personal attitude "diplomatic"; Hegel did not want to support the "opposition as it is," and thus fell into a split between his theory and practice (560); the factual difference between his theory and the existing police state was not dealt with (565). According to Ruge, it is this restriction to philosophical theory which explains why Hegel could "stand his ground" without being compelled to deny or renounce his convictions. It did not come to an open conflict because Hegel kept himself "abstractly on the side of theory" (560).

IX

On Novalis' relation to the French Revolution, see Haering, *Novalis als Philosoph*, Stuttgart 1954, pp. 484ff., and R. Samuel, *Die poetische Staats- und Geschichtsphilosophie Fr. V. Hardenbergs*, in: *Deutsche Forschungen* vol. 12, 1925.

As Haering emphasizes, for Novalis, it is a matter of "supplementing" the godless age through a "religious transcendent attitude." Critique should free the way for the coming reestablishment of religion; political revolution should pass over into a "holy revolution." However, this transition and the "plan of salvation" directed to it both presuppose that with modernity, and in the Revolution, historical development comes as such and for itself to its end, to "true anarchy" and the "annihilation of all that is positive" (*WW* ed. Wasmuth, I, 1953, p. 293), out of which religion will then rise by becoming the "new world founder." Therefore the coming renewal demands a turning away from the new age; true salvation is preserved only in the interior of subjectivity; it makes necessary a return to what is in itself past, to the orgin and to what is primal, from which the true and holy can be won back as the basis of the new world foundation. That remains typical of the romantic-aesthetic restoration up to today: The history of the modern world is a history of the decline and fall of the living orders, a decline whose overcoming is only possible in and through a return to the source. For Spengler, civilization is the form of the end and destruction of every living culture; Klages calls upon the "realm of the Pelasgians" to counter civilization and its spirit which he considers the adversary of the soul, while Heidegger appeals to the "earliest early hour" with which the "times past of the early morning of destiny" come "as the earliest time to the last . . . , that is, to bid farewell to the formerly veiled destiny of being" (*Holzwege*, 1950, p. 301).

X

The *Cours de Philosophie positive* comes to a conclusion in 1842, while the first program for it goes back to the year 1826.

In the formulation of the *Cours* (Paris 1877), the law of three stages reads as follows: "The law is this: that each of our leading conceptions—each branch of our knowledge—passes successively through three different theoretical conditions: the theological, or fictitious; the metaphysical, or abstract; and the scientific, or positive." (*August Comte and Positivism: The Essential*

Writings, ed. by Gertrude Lenzer, Harper and Row, New York, 1975, p. 71).

Although Comte wants to conceive this law as a law of human development in the generally understood sense that every human development must pass through these stages, in this natural form it is concretely a matter of interpreting the past history of humanity. The law states then that theology and metaphysics, the stages of beginning and transition, become superfluous and historical with the emergence of the positive stage (p. 77: it leaves "to them only a historical existence") and get completely supplanted by the philosophy belonging to the latter, which takes the form of science: "Having acquired the character of universality which has hitherto been the only advantage resting with the two preceding systems, it will supersede them by its natural superiority and leave to them only a historical existence" (p. 77).

Therefore for Comte the present is also the end of previous history; however, what for Novalis and the romantic restoration theories signified the fall of being that was unscathed at its origin, is for Comte the beginning of the consummation of humanity. He expressly states that the positive stage is historically definitive (77: "fully established"); henceforth, spirit can only go on progressing indefinitely in a continual enlargement of its positive knowledge (p. 77: "It can never again change its character, though it will be forever in course of development by additions of new knowledge."). With this, Comte finds the classic formulation for the principle of progress which Condorcet first posed. The epoch of humanity's consummation dawning with the present is identical to the end of previous history, which becomes relegated by it to a mere past matter.

Concerning the three stage law in detail, see L. Lévy-Bruhl, *Die Philosophie Auguste Comtes* (trans. by Molenaar), Leipzig 1902, pp. 25ff.

For the three-stage law and its fundamental meaning, so representative of the nineteenth century, it remains inessential that Comte judged the French Revolution negatively and strove to overcome the anarchy it created with his "positive philosophy." This overcoming was to be achieved by the "social physics" or sociology that he established. That says, however, that Comte saw in the society which politically constituted itself in the French Revolution the bearer of the completed development of man into humanity. Therefore the positive philosophy must go beyond the insufficient attempts of the Revolution and come to a stable progress, and in the scientific theory of society, prepare for and create the appropriate practice of its coming consummation.

XI

The text addresses essentially the first presentation of the dichotomy problem as it is definitively given in the Jena publications (prepared for by the fragmentary writings of the Bern and Frankfurt period), even though dichotomy remains the central and overriding problem of Hegelian philosophy in general. In recent Hegel literature (Löwith, Marcuse, Lukács, Bloch, Hyppolite, see the bibliographies referred to in section I of the Appendix; in addition: Th. W. Adorno and M. Horkheimer, *Dialectic of Enlightenment*, New York, 1972; Th. W. Adorno, *Minima Moralia; Reflections from Damaged Life*, London 1974) it is treated as a problem of alienation, due to the influence above all of Marx. What is important, and indeed decisive, is that one does not lose sight of the *positive* significance of dichotomy presupposed in alienation. For Hegel it is as such the historical form of unity which is not one and the sameness. In the true concept of the absolute the divine and the worldly, being and the existent, the infinite and the finite are indeed distinct from one another, yet belong in this differentiation to the absolute, whose identity thus contains and presupposes non-identity. Therefore dichotomy leads to alienation when this non-identity is removed and one of the sides is made the whole, while the other is forced into non-existence. In this manner the Enlightenment leads to alienation when it sublates the dichotomy of what is subjective and what is objective, and posits its principle of the understanding in an absolute fashion, letting perish within it what is not posited through it. Whereas the dichotomy implicitly has the function of maintaining the unity in the dirempted elements together, it becomes alienation when its contradiction is removed and a contradiction-free unity is established. Therefore, with Hegel philosophy is given the task of sublating the alienation by reclaiming from it the positivity of the dichotomy as the form of unity.

XII

Civil society gets treated independently and as a particular structure existing in its own right beside the family and the state for the first time in the *Philosophy of Right*. However, that does not mean that its problem here first becomes philosophically acute for Hegel. It rather stands constantly in his field of vision ever since his Bern period, and then always gets viewed—even already in the early *System der Sittlichkeit* (*Schr. z. Pol.*, 413 ff.)— as the elemental sphere of human action presupposed in the components of need, labor, money, property, etc., when questions of ethical life, morality (for Hegel, their separation is one of the consequences of civil society and its emancipatory positing), law, and state are dealt with. For the genesis of Hegelian social theory, besides Rosenzweig (I, 118ff., 131ff.) and Lukács, *The Young Hegel*, London 1975 (for the period up to the *Phenomenology*), reference can be made to F. Bülow, *Die Entwicklung der Hegelschen Sozialphilosophie*, Leipzig 1920 (up to the conclusion of the *Phenomenology* as well) and especially to the study of P. Vogel, *Hegels Gesellschaftsbegriff und seine geschichtliche Fortbildung durch L. v. Stein, Marx, Engels und Lassalle*, Berlin 1925.

In the more recent literature, it is true on the whole that the significance of civil society for Hegel's philosophy first begins to get fully disclosed in that literature's consideration of Marx in his relation to Hegel. See notes 4, 10, 11. In this connection, the treatment of the relationship of "lordship and bondage" in the *Phenomenology* (pp. 111ff.) has attained nothing short of classic meaning for Marx and the Marxist school. It stands as the path-breaking description and interpretation of the alienation of man which arises in modern class society; the personal ties in the relation of lordship and bondage reverse themselves and dissolve in labor and pass over into a thinglike objective relationship. For the evaluation and critique of this, see J. Kuczynski in *Deutsche Zs. f. Philos.* IV, 1956, p. 316. Marcuse also refers to it (pp. 115f.).

XIII

Almost all those works which start out from a recognition of the central position of the problem of society in Hegel's philosophy have also contributed to the analysis of the fundamental social concepts in Hegel, such as labor, the division of labor, class formation, and so forth.

Thus Marcuse writes in summary (p. 78) that "the concept of labor is not peripheral in Hegel's system, but is the central notion through which he conceives the development of society." That holds not only for the *Philosophy of Right*, but also already for the *Jena Realphilosophie* and generally for Hegel's philosophy in its entirety. From among the older works, P. Vogel's study must once again be particularly cited for its analysis of the concept of labor (Vogel, pp. 23ff.) and the expansion of society, colonization (55f.). While Hegel knows the concept of class, he lacks the concept of the proletariat, although his notion of the "rabble" bears all the characteristics that are then constitutive for the concept of the proletariat. See in this regard, H. Raupach, *Wandlung des Klassenbegriffs*, in Stud. Gen. IX, H. 4, May 1956 (pp. 222–228), which, however, does not deal with Hegel, but finds in the economic analysis, developmental historical thought, and sociological prophecy—first pursued by L. v. Stein, Marx, and Engels—the formation of the concept of class so decisive for later political and social theory. Rosenzweig (II, 123ff.) notes that Hegel's attempts to bring new meaning to the concept of estates are to be understood in connection with his consideration of the class structure of society. Concerning the concept of the proletariat, see W. Conze, *Vom "Pöbel" zum Proletariat*, in Vjschrift f. Sozial - und Wirtsch. Gesch. 41. 1954 (pp. 333–364).

XIV

For Hegel freedom is also bound up with labor, insofar as labor frees man from dependency upon nature. That makes Hegel particularly opposed to the "false" "idea" (originated by Rousseau and adopted by Romanticism) that "in respect of his needs man lived in freedom in the so-called 'state of nature,' when his needs were supposed to be confined to what are known as the simple necessities of nature" (par. 194). This notion is false precisely because it ignores "the moment of liberation intrinsic to work," intrinsic insofar as through labor, man rises out of the mere state of nature and steps into a relation to nature in which—with the predominance of tranformation of the given into his own product—the "strict natural necessity of need" recedes, and, as Hegel says, "is obscured" (par. 194). The "multiplication of needs" bound up with labor also has the same meaning of a liberation from the immediacy of nature; it contains an aspect civilizing and spiritualizing human existence insofar as it effects "a check on desire, because when many things are in use, the urge to obtain any one thing which might be needed is less strong, and this is a sign that want altogether is not so imperious" (par. 190 Addition). The result of labor is thus "refinement" (par. 191), which signifies the growth of freedom in relation to nature. Finally, labor frees man by forming him (par. 197) and producing a world which is erected as a human world by being the result of his own working on immediate nature. Labor belongs to the self-becoming of man, because in the world formed by it, he "is mainly concerned with the products of men" (par. 196).

However, for Hegel this liberation is at the same time limited within the framework of modern society by being only "abstract," that is, by tending only to "multiply and subdivide needs, means, and enjoyments indefinitely," so that together with "luxury," dependence and want increase *ad infinitum*" (par. 195) and lead to the objective independent realization of the relations of labor and means over and against direct human relations; on the other hand, the dependency of men upon one another thus increases in the form of the reification of labor, means of labor, and products of labor (par. 198), and the dependency upon nature gets replaced by dependency upon the objective relations posited in and through labor. The appearance of this reification of human relations, a reification simultaneously bound up with liberation through labor, is the "abstraction of one man's production from another's" lying in "the mechanical," which makes possible the replacement of man by the machine (par. 198).

XV

In this regard, see already the *Propadeutik* I, II par. 54, which goes back to Hegel's Nurnberg school teaching: "The state grasps society not only under legal relations, but mediates, being a truly higher moral community, the unity within custom, culture, and the general manner of thought and action" (III, 90). This early definition of the state is also only fully comprehensible in its connection to "society" when one sees it against the background of the nature theory of society, and the state it conceives as limited to this nature.

In this connection, see Marcuse (p. 61): "Hegel's demand for a strong and independent state derives from his insight into the irreconcilable contradictions of modern society." Hegel grounded its necessity upon the fact that the "antagonistic structure" of society required it. On this basis, Hegel's theory of the state can only be understood when one comprehends it in the context of civil society and its abstract ahistorical constitution. It sets free all historical and personal structures, without, however, being able to guarantee and secure them in the form of society. Therefore, the state, reduced to the sphere of society, is a "state of necessity," and this means for Hegel that the needful nature of man and labor are made the absolute standard of measure for all relations in life, or that these are left to fate, which brings them under the unlimited domination of economic interest. Civil society therefore exists historically, which is to say it exists as the reality of the entirety of human existence, only as a "state," that is, only when the right of the structures set free but not posited by society, as well as the right of the world of labor, are secured. Therefore Hegel's so-called authoritarian state has precisely the function of protecting the freedom of selfhood against society's claim for power. One could thus also say that Hegel's "state" is civil society understood in its historical character, whereas in its ahistorical abstractness it is called "society," following the usage of its economic theory.

Person and Property:
On Hegel's
Philosophy of Right,
Paragraphs 34–81 (1961)

1. Hegel treats property in the first section of the *Philosophy of Right*, entitled "Abstract Right."[1] The right in connection with which the question of property is taken up, is to begin with Roman civil law (*Privatrecht*), so far as it is defined in reference to the "utilitas singulorum," having as its object the free individual considered as a "person," in distinction from the unfree individual, that is, the individual considered in his capacity for rights. The capacity for rights here signifies that the free individual is a "person" insofar as he has the right of disposition over objects of the will, and, with this power of disposition, stands in rightful relation to other free individuals as a person. From this, Hegel concludes: The individual is a person insofar as he has the right to put his will in every object of the will, and so relate himself as "owner" of a "possession which is property" to other free individuals in their capacity as persons (pars. 40, 44). Accordingly, in the *Philosophy of Right* everything that belongs to the subjectivity of personality is excluded from the concept of the person; this remains, together with "everything which depends on particularity" a "matter of indifference" (par. 37 Addition) with regard to right for the individual as a person. With equal rigor, Hegel restricts the theory of property to that relation of persons to another by way of objects of the will which is

posited in civil law. He expressly warns against mixing in anything not having to do with the questions of property posited
through right, such as the "demand sometimes made for an
equal division of land, and other available resources too" or
"that everyone ought to have subsistence enough for his needs."
Even the question of "what and how much I possess" belongs to
"another sphere", being "a matter of indifference so far as rights
are concerned" (par. 49).[2]

What is the significance of the fact that Hegel thus brushes
aside, as "a matter of indifference so far as rights are concerned," the social problem of property which is otherwise
breaking out in the philosophical and political theory of the
time, and that he is content to take as his guide, even in detail,
the prevailing juridical theory's division of property into "taking
possession," "use of the thing," "alienation of property," and
"contract," together with all the determinations and conceptual
differentiations belonging to it?

2. The *Philosophy of Right,* as the "philosophical science of right,"
has the task of conceiving freedom as the "Idea of right" and of
presenting the "stages in the development of the Idea of the
absolutely free will" to its realization (pars. 1, 33). The possibility
of thinking freedom as the Idea of right belongs in Hegel's view
to the tradition of philosophy originating in Greece; its trans-
mission up to the threshhold of his own day takes place in the
continuing scholastic philosophy, in its derivation of a natural
right, which, deduced immediately from the nature of man
(Wolff), remains differentiated by its ground from every positive
right enacted through a "command" (iussu). Nevertheless, this
tradition first becomes the "thought of the world" where freedom no longer exists only in the thought of a pure reason di-
vorced from reality and its positive right, but rather historically
becomes the "substance of right and its goal" (par. 4) or (as He-

gel also says) the "concept" of the positive system of right itself (par. 1). With this, a system of right emerges in the world that must count, according to its principle and concept, as the "realm of freedom made actual" (par. 4).[3] As elsewhere, Hegel here excludes all postulating, projecting, and opining from philosophy; it comprehends the thought of the world and is thus, as speculative theory of right, a mere "looking on" which does "not . . . bring reason to bear on the object from the outside," but rather proceeds from the actual object which "is rational on its own account" (par. 31). "Looking on," it undertakes to follow the movement in which freedom becomes the concept of right and in which the Idea of right thus comes to realization in a positive system of right (par. 1). This observing therefore objectively presupposes that freedom has already historically become the concept of positive right: "If it is to be truly understood," the Idea "must be known both in its concept and in the determinate existence of that concept" (par. 1 Addition). Philosophy first appears as the "thought of the world" in the age following "after its process of formation has been completed" (Preface). It conceives freedom as the Idea of right after freedom has become the concept of right and the thought of the age.

3. Hegel's reference to Roman law belongs in this context; it is taken up into the speculative theory of freedom not as something historically bygone, but as the "great gift," which could already serve as the basis for the first codifications founded on rational right: the "Prussian state law,"[4] the "universal civil law code for the German fatherland" in Austria, and above all, the "Code civil des Francais." With a passionate partisanship otherwise rarely exhibited, Hegel gives his support in the *Philosophy of Right* to Thibaut and his demand for a "universal civil law code" intended to further the coalescing of the nation, to counter the trend towards "reestablishing the woolly mixture of

the old muddle" and found "our civil state of affairs in accord
with the needs of the people" and "allow the benefits of an equal
civil constitution to be bestowed upon the entire realm for eter-
nity."[5] Hegel's philosophical interpretation of Roman civil law
thus springs, as an "elevation to the universal," from the same
exigence "our time is pressing for without any limit" (par. 211
Addition) which leads to the demand for a juridical codification
of a civil code of law: "No greater insult could be offered to a
civilized people or to its lawyers than to deny them the ability to
codify their law" (par. 211). Therefore Hegel at the same time
turns sharply against Hugo's *Lehrbuch der Geschichte des Römischen
Rechts*.[6] Hugo seeks to prove the "rationality" of the historical
Roman law through the "historical method of portraying . . .
and making . . . comprehensible" its "coming to be," so as to be
at ease by means of "a good reason" in the "deduction from
conditions" with "horrible" laws and "unscrupulous and heart-
less" determinations (the right to kill debtors, slavery, children
as property of the paterfamilias, etc.), even when they fail "to
satisfy reason's most modest demands" (par. 3). Thus, for Hegel,
reference to Roman civil law is a positive concern to the degree
that it has become the basis for contemporary legislation. He
takes up the question of what becomes the foundation of right
with the advent of political revolution and the emergence of
civil society. In this upheaval the concepts of Roman law are
melted down and filled with the substance that belongs to the
contemporary world. Whereas in the historical Roman law "person" still designated a particular class of men, that included in
its "right of the particular person" the "right over slaves" and
"family relationships" entailing "the status of having lost one's
rights" (par. 40), with the advent of modern civil society the
right of the person as such, and therewith the capacity for rights
of man as man, that is, of all men, is posited; and freedom is
elevated without restriction to the principle and concept of

right. Hegel proceeds from this in his description of the civil administration of justice belonging to civil society: "It is part of education, of thinking as the consciousness of the single in the form of universality, that the ego comes to be apprehended as a universal person in which all are identical. A man counts as a man in virtue of his manhood alone, not because he is a Jew, Catholic Protestant, German, Italian, etc." (par. 209). With this, freedom, as the freedom of all, becomes the concept of right; it has come to "hold valid"; it has attained "objective reality." The world history of freedom beginning in Greece has turned to its consummation in civil society and its right. What counted in the thought of rational right only as the Idea of right in itself has now worked itself into political reality; it becomes the concept and principle of all positive right. With this, every positive, historically emergent right loses its right to the degree that it contradicts the principle of freedom and of human rights. For Hegel, the playing out of the "good old right" against the "Idea" that has become the "concept of right" reveals the impotence of restoration; as the "extreme" of "rigid adherence to the . . . law of a bygone situation," it is only the "opposite of what started twenty-five years ago in a neighboring realm and what at the time re-echoed in all heads; namely, that in a political constitution nothing should be recognized as valid unless its recognition accorded with the right of reason."[7]

4. In starting from Roman law as the basis of civil right and then proceeding in its exposition from the foundation of freedom, the *Philosophy of Right* can be understood as the philosophical theory of the realization of freedom, conceived as the actual existence of all as free individuals. This makes it necessary for Hegel to go beyond the natural and rational right theories of Scholasticism, though he has recourse to them, in order to take up the question of the immanent reason of the contemporary upheaval. Its "relation to reality," defined by the separation of rational right from positive right, has now become a "misunderstanding"; what counts is "wrenching" philosophy out of this misunderstanding and returning to the truth "that, since philosophy is the exploration of the rational, it is for that very reason the apprehension of the present and the actual" (Preface). This determines in substance the task of the *Philosophy of Right* in relation to the upheaval of the contemporary age. It leaves behind every type of immediate deduction of rules of right from the Idea. Where freedom has become the concept of right, it is no longer a question of conceiving it in the in-itselfness of possibility, but in its realization. Freedom, which could only be thought as belonging "in itself" to the nature of man in the natural right theory of Scholasticism, has now historically emerged from the state of "possibility" into actual existence. In starting from the "will," which "is free," the *Philosophy of Right* therefore undertakes to conceive the "system of right" as the "realm of freedom made actual" (par. 4). With this it brings to determination the foundation upon which the right posited with civil society is grounded. Everything that the *Philosophy of Right* successively handles in the "stages in the development of the Idea"—abstract right, morality, marriage, family, society, and the state as administration and rule—thus belongs to the theory of freedom and its realization. Whereas the natural right discussion up to today has been unable to break through the abstract concept of human nature, which is limited to the "in itself" or immediate natural being, Hegel on the contrary conceives the realization of freedom in the context of the entire ethical spiritual world emerging in world history. He grasps what has become the substance of all legal and political order, contemporary with the political revolution's principle of freedom and right, not in the element of postulation and what ought to be, but rather concretely as a "world-historical condition."[8]

5. Hegel's theory of property belongs in this context. Unlike all attempts in this period to derive property from a construction of its original emergence or, as in scholastic philosophy, deductively from human nature, the *Philosophy of Right*, as an "apprehension of the present," starts out from the relation posited in civil law in which free individuals are connected to one another as persons by way of objects of the will standing as property.[9] However, here lies the difficulty as well. The freedom based on property which Hegel places at the beginning of the movement which leads to the realization of freedom has all substantial relations of humanness outside it. Personal right therefore gets termed "abstract right" by Hegel; the "external sphere" of freedom (par. 41) posited with property is, as the "opposite of what is substantive" (par. 42), only something "formal" (par. 37). However, that does not now mean that one has to go beyond the property of civil right to morality, family, society, and state in order to come to something essential. In this manner one leaves out the decisive thesis of the *Philosophy of Right*, that all substantial spiritual-ethical orders of freedom also come into existence with the property of civil right. With this, the abstract external sphere of property posited in abstract right is understood by Hegel as the condition of the possibility for the realization of freedom in the entire range of its religious, political, and ethical substance. The freedom of man, as the freedom belonging to European world history, is brought to its determinate being in the abstract freedom of property: "The freedom which we have here is what is called a person, that is, the subject who is free, free indeed in his own eyes, and who gives himself an embodiment in things" (par. 33 Addition). Hegel was the first in Germany to comprehend that the coming civil society would

establish itself in the "amassing of wealth" and in the "dependence and distress of the class tied to work" (par. 243), through
an upheaval of all historical relations by the property relations
it posited. Nevertheless, he can say that with civil property,
Christian freedom comes into existence: "It is about a millen-
nium and a half since the freedom of personality began through
the spread of Christianity to blossom and gain recognition as a
universal principle from a part, though still a small part, of the
human race. But it was only yesterday, we might say, that the
principle of freedom of property became recognized in some
places. This example from history may serve to rebuke the im-
patience of opinion and to show the length of time that mind
requires for progress in its self-consciousness" (par. 62). So Hegel conceives the freedom which civil right posits in property as
the determinate being of freedom in all stages of its realization.
The meaning of this reference of its historical and metaphysical
substance to the abstract property of civil right separated from
it is then later partly rejected as speculative inversion, and partly
no longer understood, so that it is allowed to vanish altogether.

If one asks for the basis of this reference, it emerges from the
fact that Hegel, in conceiving what is, refrains from taking from
the freedom of right any of its abstractness or from adding anything to it. In letting it stand and getting to the bottom of it
through laying it out, he brings to its concept what the connection of the person's freedom to objects of the will as property
makes necessary and what thus is its truth.

6. The abstractness of freedom in civil law rests upon the fact
that the free individual—here not the "personality," man in the
entire breadth of his humanness—is the person who gives himself "an external sphere" of freedom (par. 41) and so "is here
realized first of all in an external thing" (par. 41 Addition). With
regard to right, an object of the will is every corporeal thing (res

corporalis), insofar as it can stand in relations of right. The object of the will and thus property therefore get defined in that they are "what is immediately different from free mind," "something not free, not personal, without rights" (par. 42). Whereas in historical Roman law the person still was a particular class and so men could also be taken as objects of the will and unfree entities, modern civil right allows only natural things and what can be taken as something "external" and "not personal" to count as objects of the will (par. 42). However, that does not mean that it is possible to equate objects of the will with natural things. These become objects of the will only when they can enter into relations of right and so stand at the disposal of man, whereas everything natural which is fundamentally outside the disposition of men, like the sun and stars, remain likewise non-objects of the will.

Hegel takes this up in order to lead the thus determined, pre-given concept of the object of the will back into the movement which has become fixed in it. All property that man can have as an object of the will for his own, presupposes in itself the action and the acting grip of man, with which the natural is torn from its independence and brought under the disposition of man. Behind the seeming thinglike fixedness that property has as an object of the will, lies concealed for Hegel the movement, the often long historical process of the active preparation of nature, with which it gets transformed into an object of the will and taken into possession by man as an object of the will. Therefore "taking possession," in which I bring a natural entity under my external "power" (pars. 45, 56), is entailed in the object of the will as property. Hegel takes this up, like all the other traditional subdivisions of property into corporeal possession-taking, formation, marking, use of the object of the will, etc., because they contain the truth that all objects of the will as property are "realized and actualized" only in what man does with them in appropriating, transforming, and using them (see par. 59). Where therefore the object of the will is immediately taken as a natural thing, the fact that the nature which becomes the object of the will has no substance or independence in itself is ignored. This nature receives its determination in man's grip; in that he puts his will in it, it obtains an end which it does not have "in itself" (par. 44). Hegel has therefore called "formation" the "taking possession most in conformity with the Idea" (par. 56). In it is "subjectively" presupposed that all the forms of action are developed by which man grasps, alters, and so forms nature into an object of the will, first in an immediate corporeal way, then in the extension of the hand, "that magnificent tool which no animal possesses" (par. 55 Addition), through "mechanical forces, weapons, tools" (par. 55). However, with this "subjective" element the "objective" element is at the same time united: In the "tilling of the soil, the cultivation of plants, the taming and feeding of animals," and in the "contrivances for utilizing raw materials or the forces of nature," what I can do to nature does not remain "external" to it; it is "assimilated" by it and thereby becomes a determination through which the nature formed into an object of the will is distinguished in itself from the same nature which, undisturbed by such formation, is not in the hands and disposition of man (par. 56). Therefore, in Hegel's view, no philosophy can comprehend the formed nature and the relations of man to nature based upon it if it proceeds from a nature which stands independently over and against man and is thus supposed to be immediately given to his intuition and representation. It remains blind in face of its own historical presuppositions; it does not see that nature is first able to be an object when it has become an object of the will and man has therewith become its subject: "The so-called 'philosophy' which attributes reality in the sense of self-subsistence and genuine independent self-enclosed existence to unmediated single things, to the nonpersonal, is directly contradicted by the free will's attitude to these things . . . While so-called 'external' things have a show of self-subsistence for consciousness, intuition, and representive thinking, the free will idealizes that type of actuality and so is its truth" (par. 44). This truth is the historical relation skipped over in such philosophy and excluded from consideration by the acceptance of a constant subject-object relation, the historical relation in which nature ceases to be the "immediate given world" and is formed by man into the nature which, as an object of the will in his hands, has left but the "semblance of independence," because it is, as his object, the world in which man has presence without still being present himself "here and now" (par. 56). In his handwritten notations to his lectures, Hegel writes: "Man is master over everything in nature, only through him is there determinate being as determinate being of freedom . . . only man is free" (Hoffmeister p. 327). The symbolic form of marking property present since ancient times is explained in the same sense: The "mark" on the object of the will, put there by man, shows what is essential. The marked entity no longer counts as that which it is; "by being able to give a mark to things and thereby to acquire them, man . . . shows his mastery over things" (pars. 58, 58 Addition). Therefore, in Hegel's view, there is no longer any possibility of deriving freedom from the state of nature of man or from an ahistorical constant concept of nature. The truth of abstract civil right, and of its freedom which is limited to the relation of persons to factors, is grounded herein: Man, who, as a natural being, is free only "according to the concept," only "implicitly" and "potentially," can first become free *in actu* when he frees himself from the unfreedom of the state of nature and makes nature an object of the will, breaking its power. The "position of the free will, with which right and the science of right begin" is therefore fundamentally "in advance of the false position at which man" is taken "as a natural entity and only the concept implicit" (par. 57).[10] The freedom of the person and the determination of nature as object of the will belong inextricably together. For Hegel, there is no possibility of arguing over freedom and unfreedom with reasons and counter-arguments which are taken from the nature of man: Freedom exists historically and *in actu* only where man has put the state of nature behind and so no longer remains a natural being in relation to a nature that has power over him. "The alleged justification of slavery (by reference to all its proximate beginnings through physical force, capture in war, saving and preservation of life, upkeep, education, philanthropy, the slave's own acquiescence, and so forth) . . . and all historical views of the justice of slavery and lordship, depend on regarding man as a natural entity pure and simple, as an existent not in conformity with its concept" (par. 57). The same holds for all attempts to derive lordship from the natural law of natural superiority, power, and strength. For this reason, Hegel attacked the "crudity" of v. Haller's political theory, which vindicates "the rule of the mightier" because it supposedly corresponds to the "order of nature" as the "everlasting ordinance of God." With this, the principle of right is made victim of the order of nature in accord with which "the vulture rends the innocent lamb" and "the mighty are quite right to treat their unsuspecting clients as the weak and . . . empty their pockets." In this manner one passes off "absurdity . . . as the word of God" (par. 258). Where freedom becomes actual in the right of the person to objects of the will, all forms of "rule" based upon man's natural condition and the order of nature become an injustice. Rule in the form of the state presupposes the freedom of right, that man can no longer be taken as a natural being (par. 57). Therefore the relationship in which persons give themselves a determinate being in objects of the will is the commencement of freedom. For Hegel, however, this at the same time entails, in positive terms, the insight that the universal freedom of civil right can only be realized on the basis of civil society, because only with its rational rule over nature does the history of man's liberation from the power of nature come to its conclusion through nature's thoroughgoing determination as object of the will. Therefore the *Philosophy of Right* opposes the world-historical positivity of the rational domination of nature to every theory that seeks to devalue modern society and civilization as the decline and fall of an original holy humanness, such as Hegel encountered in Rousseauianism and in the romantic poetization of origins and of an immediate original nature, as if "man lived in freedon in the so-called 'state of nature.'" Insofar as such an idea ignores the "moment of liberation intrinsic to work" (par. 194), it remains blind to the fact that man is only able to be free *in actu* where nature is determined as object of the will and, as the object of human disposition, has become the property of man. Thus, in Hegel's view, the existence of freedom is tied to the practical liberation of man from the power of nature. The insight, which he therewith attains in the age of emerging civil society, has for itself—still today in opposition to every form of theory of decline—the power of the elementary truth that the right posited together with human right, the right of all men to the freedom of humanness, is irreducibly tied to modern society and its rational domination of nature. With this insight, it at the same time becomes comprehensible why, in the process of modernization finally sweeping over the entire globe, machines, tractors, and power stations could become symbols of freedom, which call forth the passion of concern more than do the isolated political and cultural freedoms taken in their own right. These have no concrete existence without the determination of nature as object of the will presupposed in the property relation and without the overcoming of all dependency stemming from the state of nature, an overcoming made possible by this determination. Hegel was the first in

Germany at that time to see this and grasp it as the truth of civil law and its abstract freedom, limited to the relations of persons to objects of the will taken as property.

7. This freedom, however, at the same time entails that with it individuals as persons—limited to the relation to objects of the will—"exist for each other" only by means of objects of the will and so "only as owners" (par. 40). The mediation of all relations of persons to persons through objects of the will is the other side of property. On the basis of civil society, this does not remain limited to the relation of external natural things. It equally entails that all capacities and talents of the person can be depersonalized and take on the form of "objects of the will" at all levels of ability and so function socially as "property." This holds without restriction on the basis of civil society. All "mental aptitudes, erudition, artistic skill, even things ecclestiastical (like sermons, mass . . .), inventions," . . . "attainments, aptitudes, etc." become subject to determination as objects of the will like external things and so get "brought on to a parity, through being bought and sold" as "subjects of contract" and "recognized" objects of the will. Hegel does remark that one would perhaps take exception to directly calling them "objects of the will"; nevertheless, it is here the case that even what is "something internal" for men gets "alienated" and becomes "something external," whereby it can be brought under the determination of the object of the will (par. 43). For Hegel, the universal principle of civil society lies in such mediation of all relations through objects of the will. The relation to nature constitutive for it also draws under its sway individuals as persons. Therefore the universal of civil society steps forward in a rightful manner in contract, insofar as its "sphere . . . is made up of this mediation whereby I hold property not merely by means of a thing and my subjective will and so hold it in virtue of my participation in a common will" (par. 71). The "mediation" that so attains a rightful form in contract is, on the one hand, the positive aspect of civil society: through the determination of things as objects of the will it has as its subject the "concrete person who is himself the object of his particular aims" (par. 182); as "private persons," its individuals are bourgeois "whose end is their own interest" (par. 187). Therefore Hegel calls it "the true and proper ground in which freedom is existent" (par. 71). However, for him, it is at the same time the power of "division" and "difference" (par. 33, 182 Addition) in virtue of its mediation of all relations through objects of the will and their reduction to an intercourse restricted to buying, selling, earning, alienating, and trading. This power detaches the social existence of individuals in themselves and in their relations to one another from all substantial, personal, and ethical ties, and in this separation posits the "actual attainment of selfish ends" as the sole universal social principle, according to which "each member is his own end, everything else is nothing to him" (par. 183, 182, 182 Addition). The "particularity" of individuals "given free rein in every direction to satisfy their needs, accidental caprices, and subjective desires" can destroy "itself and its substantive concept" in this abstractness of an externalized being determined as an object of the will in which "civil society" can afford "a spectacle of extravagance and want as well as of the physical and ethical degeneration common to them both" (par. 185). One can already find in Hegel all those features which can be taken as the reification and destruction of every human personal bond, and then played off against civil society and its individual freedom, which "permits no other bond than naked interest" (*Communist Manifesto*). Whereas revolutionary theory is here led to posit the liberation from nature as the true social core of the freedom constitutive for civil society, and to play this off against the form of its property, Hegel insists nevertheless that property must have the "character of private property" (par. 46). He thereby goes beyond, as it were, the negativity that it also signifies for him to maintain that the relationship of persons limited to objects of the will is not only the condition of liberation from nature, but simultaneously the positive condition of the freedom of individuals: In property "my will, as the will of a person, and so as a single will, becomes objective" (par. 46), in that "I am myself an immediate individual" (par. 47) and "I as free will am an object to myself" (par. 45). In the context of the *Philosophy of Right*, it is unmistakably clear that in civil society the "self-subsistent inherently infinite personality of the individual" comes as such to its realization. This is expressly stated; for the very first time in history civil right gives "the development of particularity to self-subsistance" its right, with which "Plato . . . could only cope" by excluding it, "even in its very beginnings in private property and the family," from his "purely substantial state" (par. 185).[11]

For Hegel, the abstract determination of things as objects of the will in which civil society restricts itself to the relation of man to nature and creates the condition of freedom in the transforming of nature, thus has at the same time the further significance of—now in the externalization of all relations of persons to one another—producing freedom in the total range of its world-historical substance, bringing it to the form of "world spirit" (par. 4) and giving personality as person the freedom in which it can exist as itself. The externality of civil society, which, on the one hand, offers the spectacle of extravagance and want, is for Hegel, on the other hand, the existence of individual freedom.

8. Whereas the dichotomy thus constitutive for society later becomes the problem whose solution is supposed to win back the unity of man's being, lost in the dichotomy, by negating either the substantial historical condition or the society cast in its spiritless non-being, Hegel comprehends that the abstractness, mediation through objects of the will, and externalization of all relations is inherently, as dichotomy, the power of the positive and the negative at one and the same time. The same movement in which society restricts itself to the world of objects of the will and thereby socially detaches man from his historical being, has as much the infinitely positive consequence that personality enters into society and its functions only as person and property owner and can thereby become the subject of all the realms of inner and ethical human existence that society sets outside itself. Hegel has shown what this means in the rightful form of alienation constitutive for property. It implies, for one thing, that the possibility of my withdrawing my will from them is entailed in the object of the will and in the relations mediated by objects of the will (see par. 65). However, with this a second element is given: on the basis of modern civil society and with its right, in which all persons are fundamentally differentiated from objects of the will, alienation presupposes the inalienability of the person himself in the determinacy that the person may have his own inner and external being for himself unimpeached by society. Therefore, for Hegel, in distinction from all premodern legal orders which always stand upon substantial religious and personal bonds, those goods become inalienably my own "which constitute my own private personality and the universal essence of my self-consciousness," such as "my personality as such, my universal freedom of will, my ethical life, my religion" (par. 66). Here lies the reason why, in Hegel's view, the freedom of property is the principle with which Christian freedom first of all achieves existence: Since society restricts itself to the relations of persons to one another mediated through property, it liberates the individual as personality to become subject in everything which constitutes the wealth and depth of the personal, ethical, spiritual being that is now untouched by any determination as object of the will.

9. Therefore Hegel also saw in the determination of the labor relation as an object of the will the decisive principle which comprises the "distinction . . . between a slave and a modern domestic servant or day-laborer" (par. 67 Addition). Their freedom consists in that what they reduce to an "object of the will" and can "alienate" in the rightful form of contract is not themselves but only their labor power and the use of their skills for a limited time. Thereby the inalienability of personality in its own sphere becomes an insurmountable restriction and every form of state of nature domination becomes an injustice. "Single products of my particular physical and mental skill and of my power to act I can alienate to someone else and I can give him the use of my abilities for a restricted period, because, on the strength of this restriction, my abilities acquire an external relation to the totality and universality of my being" (par. 67; compare par. 80). With this, freedom becomes for the first time without restriction the principle of a society. As a world of labor mediated through objects of the will, modern society frees man not only from the power of nature, but simultaneously elevates freedom to the universal principle through the determination of labor and of all labor relations in such a form that skills can only be alienated as objects of the will and property for a limited time; it releases to the person in himself, as personality, his selfhood and its realization. Therefore employer and laborer also no longer act towards one another as master and slave in the state of nature, but as persons. That is for Hegel the rational meaning of modern labor relations; with them, the freedom of all makes itself prevail—although at first in the form of misery. The free individual as person attains the freedom, transcending society and its world of objects of the will, to have his life as his own and to be himself as personality. For Hegel, this is grounded in the principle of right of person and property; it brings into existence the Idea of freedom in relation to all men as persons. With the dichotomy in the form of the determination of objects of the will constituting civil society, all individuals become, as bearers of personality, subjects of the human spiritual world in its entire wealth, mediated through the world-historical tradition.[12]

10. Therefore "the classification of rights (adopted by Kant and since favored by others) into *jus reale*, *jus personale*, and *jus realiter personale*," that is, into rights involving objects of the will, and personal and thinglike-personal rights,[13] is rejected by Hegel as a "confusion" (par. 40). By accepting it, one ignores the fact that with civil right the freedom of personality comes into existence in person and property. Consequently, when there is a "disorderly intermixture of rights which presuppose substantial ties, for example, those of family and political life, and rights that only concern abstract personality as such," then the sense of personhood, which points beyond society and its abstract determination of objects of the will is precisely left out of consideration. For this reason, Hegel conceives right concerning objects of the will as personal right; with it, the "right of the person as person" is recognized (par. 40). Because civil society posits itself as the world of objects of the will, whose subjects are all individuals existing as persons, it is, in its consummation of the liberation of man from nature and as the power of difference and division, the condition which allows man as man, for the first time in the history of humanity, to be "personality"; and thus finally to give himself and freedom a determinate being and reality in the wealth of the historically formed human being encompassing the horizon of all cultures.

Notes

1. The *Philosophy of Right* [*Grundlinien der Philosophie des Rechts*] is cited according to the edition of J. Hoffmeister (Hamburg 1955). Hoffmeister takes as his basis the text which Hegel himself allowed to be printed in 1820 out of the "need for putting into the hands of my audience a text-book for the lectures on the Philosophy of Right which I deliver in the course of my professional duties"; he adds to it the handwritten notes "which Hegel apparently made for him to serve as aids for expanded discussion and explanation in the delivery of the lecture." The book is thus a "manual" and "compendium"; it leaves aside everything "which would receive its requisite elucidation in my lectures" (*Philosophy of Right*, p. 1). Hegel had already lectured on "Natural Right and Political Science" in Berlin during the winter of 1818–1819, before the publication of his manual; how Hegel then proceeded in his lectures is documented by an extant transcript (for the reference to which I thank Dr. F. Nicolin); he dictated the paragraphs, in order then to elucidate them in free expositions and further develop in particular the relationships which touch upon the connection between what is densely summarized in the paragraphs and the contemporary reality and its political as well as philosophical theories, etc. Therefore, so long as the critical edition (prepared by the Hegel Archive in Bonn) of all the available transcripts of the lectures held with the guide of the compendium (1821/22; 1822/23; 1824/25) is still outstanding, there can be no dispensing with the "Additions" which E. Gans compiled from the lecture transcripts and appended to the paragraphs in his edition of the *Philosophy of Right* (vol. 8 of the *Werke* edited from 1832–1840 by "an association of friends of the immortal man")—as justified as Hoffmeister's critique of Gans's selection procedure certainly is (see p. xiiff. of his edition). The "Additions" are cited according to vol. 7 of the Stuttgart *Jubiläumsausgabe*, published by H. Glockner from 1927 on.

It is striking how little attention has been paid to Hegel's theory of civil law and the private property belonging in its sphere, even by the literature on Hegel's *Philosophy of Right*. This is essentially due to the fact that for quite some time now the speculative (metaphysical) theory of right has been something foreign to legal science and has attracted interest to itself with respect to its universal foundation as such. Therefore the theory of property is mostly treated in the literature only as an element and component within the general, systematic context of the Hegelian philosophy of right. See Binder, Busse, and Larenz, "Hegels Dialektik des Willens und das Problem der juristischen Persönlichkeit," *Logos* 20 (1931), 196ff.; by the same authors, "Hegel und das Privatrecht," *Verh. d. 2. Hegel Kongresses* (1931), published by v. B. Wigersma, Tübingen and Haarlem 1932, pp. 135ff.; A. Trott zu Solz, *Hegels Staatsphilosophie und das Internationale Recht*, Göttingen 1932, pp. 34f.; J. Binder, *Grundlegung zur Rechtsphilosophie*, Tübingen 1935, pp. 98ff., above all pp. 102f.; A. Poggi, "La filosofia giuridica di Hegel," *Riv. Int. di. Filos. del Diritto* 15, (1935), 43ff.; with regard to Hegel's natural right, see F. Darmstädter, "Das Naturrecht als soziale Macht und die Rechtsphilosophie Hegels," *Sophia* 4 (1936), 181–190, 421–444; 5 (1937), 212–235.

2. Because civil society is the "battlefield" of "individual private interest," (par.

289) and in its emancipatory abstractness has outside itself the sphere of personal being, "the specific characteristics pertaining to private property may . . . be subordinated to a higher sphere of right (e.g. to a society or the state)." However, such "exceptions . . . cannot be grounded in chance, in private caprice, or private advantage, but only in the rational organism of the state" (par. 46). In his lectures, Hegel has expressly added that it is "only the state that can do this" (par. 46 Addition). For Hegel, the irrevocable presupposition of the modern state always remains that freedom comes to realization in it, as does therewith "my will" as the "will of a person," the "person" as a "this." Therein lies the necessity of private property, which, in the determination "of being 'this' or 'mine'" (par. 46 Addition), thus also remains the presupposition in all the transformations and changes that property undergoes within the context of the development of society and state.

3. With the *Philosophy of Right* as a "compendium" for the lectures which he delivers in the course of his "professional duties," Hegel expressly harks back to the "natural law" of scholastic philosophy in its systematic grounding through the "philosophia practica universalis" (Christian Wolff, *Philosophica practica universalis* 1738–1739 and frequently thereafter; *Jus naturae methodo scientifica pertractatum* 1740–1748 T. 1–8). This is indicated by its subtitle, "Natural Law and Political Science in Outline." Through this reference, Hegel determines the task of his own philosophy. Whereas philosophy "was with the Greeks for instance, pursued in private like an art," it now "has an existence in the open, in contact with the public, and especially, or even only, in the service of the state" (p. 7). This determination, that the Philosophy of Right be "philosophy in the service of the state," has brought upon Hegel the well-known political accusations that he gave the spirit of Prussian reaction a scientific dwelling in his philosophy and so forth (Haym). In actual fact, Hegel here states only that in the newly founded Berlin University, philosophy has in general secured its place at the university as a "post," just as it has in our day. This post, however, presupposes not any direction of teaching by the government, but precisely that "governments have proved their trust in their scholars who have made philosophy their chosen field by leaving entirely to them the construction and contents of philosophy" (p. 7); as the appointers, they can thereby have absolutely no further knowledge concerning why philosophy has a place in the state-supported university, nor concerning what belongs together with philosophy and in its teaching; their trust can be the "indifference to learning itself" which retains "professional chairs of philosophy . . . only as a tradition" (p. 7). Hegel thus determines his own philosophy as "academic philosophy," in reference to his post as well as to state service; it thereby obtains the substantial task of harking back to the tradition of Greek philosophy, which "continues to spin its thread" as a "scholastic wisdom" to the "good fortune of the sciences" at the university. His philosophy is to retrieve this tradition from its state of decay and termination and call it back into the present, so as to place it in a relation to contemporary reality, which has been lost for itself and for the consciousness of the age through the separation of pure thought from the givenness abandoned to the experience of empiricism for which "the ontology, rational psychology, cosmology, yes even natural theol-

Notes

ogy, of former times" may no longer be considered (*Science of Logic*, preface, p. 25). Already in a letter of 1816 to Friedrich v. Raumer (August 2, 1816), Hegel dissociated himself from the prevailing opinion that in philosophy, "the determinacy and diversity of information" is "superfluous for the Idea, and indeed, contrary to and beneath it," and wrote in opposition that what really counted is shaping "the wide field of objects which belong to philosophy into an ordered whole built through its parts" (*WG* 3, 319). In this manner Hegel renews scholastic and academic philosophy with his own philosophy. However, that does not mean that Hegel seeks to undo the "break" that has taken place. With the political upheaval of the age, and in the "complete transformation which philosophical thought in Germany has undergone in the last twenty-five years," a new principle and a "higher standpoint" (*Science of Logic*, p. 25) has taken shape. Past philosophies cannot be "woken again"; "mummies when brought amongst living beings cannot there remain." The call "to revert to the standpoint of an ancient philosophy" is the "escape of an incapacity" (*Lectures on the History of Philosophy*, vol. I, pp. 46–47). Therefore the reference to scholastic philosophy in its terminal form has the meaning of incorporating the tradition preserved within it into the higher standpoint of the new principle; in its old task of grounding "the rational," it should be brought to "the apprehension of the present and the actual" (*Philosophy of Right*, Preface, p. 10), and thereby to satisfy the "demand" of "the rich material" of the present "which demands to be controlled and comprehended in its very depths by thought" (*Lectures on the History of Philosophy*, vol. I, pp. 47, 48). In this general determination, Hegel's *Philosophy of Right* is the renewed "universal practical philosophy" of the eighteenth-century school (that of Christian Wolff in particular) and of its doctrinal traditions going back to the ethics and "politics" of Aristotle. Concerning Christian Wolff's "philosophia practica universalis" in its relation to Aristotle, see Joachim Ritter, "'Naturrecht' bei Aristoteles" in Joachim Ritter, *Metaphysik und Politik*, pp. 133ff.

4. In Bern Hegel had already thoroughly dealt with Prussian common law in connection with his then extensive historical and political studies, characterized by the "insatiable hunger for facts and information" manifest in them; see Fr. Rosenzweig, *Hegel und der Staat*, Munich 1920, vol. I, pp. 30ff.; Th. Haering, *Hegel, sein Wollen und sein Werk*, 1929, vol. I. pp. 124f. Through H. Thiele (and others, *Die preussische Kodifikation*, Privatrechtl. Stud. II, ZRG, Germ. Abt. 57, 1937), Fr. Wieacker (*Privatrechtsgeschichte der Neuzeit*, Göttingen 1952), above all, however, through the publication of the "Vorträge über Recht und Staat von Carl Gottlieb Suarez" (Wiss. Abh. d. AG. f. Forschg. d. Landes Nordrhein-Westfalen, vol. 10, Opladen 1960) overseen by von H. Conrad and G. Kleinheyer (see H. Conrad, *Die geistigen Grundlagen des Allgemeinen Landrechts f. d. preuss. Staaten* [AG. f. Forschg. Geisteswissenschaften, H. 77], Opladen, 1958), the preconditions have now finally been established for investigating the as yet thoroughly unclarified relation between the philosophy of right (not only of Hegel) to the concrete development of right of the epoch. At that time, the connection to the natural-law theory of philosophy is always presupposed in it; Dilthey has shown that in the case of Prussian common law: "Natural law provides it its principles and Roman law . . . becomes, in its legal propositions and concepts, the juridical

instrument of its work." (See "Das Allgemeine Landrecht" in: *Ges. W.*, vol. 12, p. 2; Stuttgart and Göttingen edition 1960, p. 148).

5. A. F. Thibaut, "Über die Notwendigkeit eines Allgemeinen Bürgerlichen Rechts für Deutschland," 1814, in: *Thibaut und Savigny*, edited and introduced by J. Stern, Berlin 1914 (photo-offset reprint), Darmstadt 1959, pp. 41 and 47.

6. Gustav Hugo, *Lehrbuch eines zivilistischen Kurses, Vol. III: Lehrbuch der Geschichte des Römischen Rechts bis auf Justinian*, 1799, 1806, 1810, 1815, 1818, 1820, and frequently thereafter, see Note 11, 1832, pp. viiiff.

Hegel's critique of this manual comprises his fundamental coming to grips with the historical school of law. After the philosophy of right of Scholasticism had separated the concept of right founded on human nature from positive law, and after the difference of the latter from natural law or "law from a philosophical point of view" was subsequently perverted "into an opposition and a contradiction," the historical school of right has, in Hegel's eyes, undertaken to make the philosophical concept superfluous and to replace it by "knowledge, based on proximate or remote historical causes." This "purely historical task . . . is appreciated and rewarded in its own sphere"; the misunderstanding therefore lies in its claim to take over the tasks of philosophical theory and thereby stretch "historical explanation and justification . . . to become an absolutely valid justification." Where this occurs, "the relative is put in the place of the absolute and the external appearance in place of the true nature of the thing" (par. 3, p. 17ff.). It is characteristic of Hegel's relation to v. Savigny, who had already occupied the chair of Roman law when Hegel was appointed at Berlin, that Hegel avoids mentioning him here in this context. With regard to the objective presuppositions of the conflict between the "two Berlin colleagues Savigny and Hegel," a conflict "partly degenerating into personal antagonism," see R. Schmidt, *Die Rückkehr zu Hegel and die strafrechtliche Verbrechenslehre*, Stuttgart 1913, pp. 22ff. Lenz reports on the conflict which then broke out with the appointment of Hegel's student, E. Gans, and finally led to v. Savigny withdrawing himself entirely from the affairs of his department, in *Geschichte der Universität zu Berlin*, Halle 1910, II, 1 pp. 390ff.; see in this regard the collection of the documents relevant to the dispute in vol. IV, No. 186–194 and 233–243.

7. *Proceedings of The Estates Assembly in Wurtemberg, Hegel's Political Writings*, pp. 281, 282. For Hegel, it fundamentally holds true that age is no principle of right. "An actual positive right a hundred years old rightly perishes if the basis conditioning its existence disappears" (*ibid.*, p. 283). see on this point *The German Constitution* of 1802 in *Hegel's Political Writings*, p. 146 and elsewhere.

8. With his theory of the realization of freedom and human nature as well, Hegel takes up the core of Aristotle's practical philosophy; see in this regard, Ritter, "'Naturrecht' bei Aristoteles," pp. 146ff., 166ff. In par. 4, the reference back to the Aristotelian concept of actualized nature as something distinct from nature as possibility is immediately overlaid with the determination that the "world of spirit" is a "second nature," compare Aristotle's *Politics*, I, 2 1252b 32–34; see

also in this regard par. 10 of the *Philosophy of Right*: "The Understanding goes no further than the purely implicit character of a thing and consequently calls the freedom which accords with this implicit character a 'potency,' because if freedom is only implicit it is indeed mere potentiality"; however, it can thereby look upon its "reality" only as an "application to a given material, not belonging to the essence of freedom itself." In his lectures, Hegel elucidated this with the example of a child: "The child is man implicit. At first it possesses reason only implicitly; it begins by being the potentiality of reason and freedom, and so is free only in accordance with its concept." To this he added the general notion that "what exists purely implicitly in this way does not yet exist in its actuality" (see par. 10 Addition). The Aristotelian doctrine of the realization of nature as "praxis" remains at least formally contained in practical philosophy up until the eighteenth century; it is found prior to Hegel in Christian Wolff; see *Ph. pr. univ.* par. 122: quiquid naturaliter possibile est . . . ad actum perducitur; actions (actiones) of man are thus in themselves by nature directed to the full realization of the possibilities given in his nature (perfectio), see I par. 103. However, in the deductive scholastic theory, which sets itself off from experience and historical reality, this realization is restricted to "morality" conceived as the merely inner determination of action, as Kant retained it. In contrast, Hegel conceives the institutional, ethical, social, and political reality as the "realm of freedom made actual" and thereby reinstates the Aristotelian doctrine that the nature of man does not come to its realization "by nature" but ethically-politically in the polis and as the polis.

9. It is generally peculiar to Hegel's philosophy that it does not do away with or replace the theories preceding it, but rather sublates them. It thus "prevents" the "hardening and isolation of individual principles and their systems" in order to counteract the tendency of the part "to constitute itself a whole and an absolute", see G. W. F. Hegel, *Natural Law: The Scientific Ways of Treating Natural Law, Its Place in Moral Philosophy, and Its Relation to the Positive Sciences of Law*, translated by T. M. Knox, University of Pennsylvania Press, Philadelphia 1975, p. 124. Thus one finds incorporated as elements in his theory of property the natural-right foundation proceeding from Locke, which involves the derivation from labor decisive for political economy, legal theory in the sense of Montesquieu, and also Fichte's determination of property, which diverges from the labor principle by conceiving property as the basic right of the person according to the "principle of all considerations of right," that all property is based "upon the union of the wills of the many into one will" (Fichte, *Grundlage d. Naturrechts WW*, published by v. Medicus, vol. 2, pp. 133f., 116, 216ff.). Since Hegel gets his own standpoint by making philosophy the comprehension of existing reason as the historically present reality, the adopted theories are unified in the task of *hermeneutically* determining the property emergent in world history, and now posited with civil society and its right of the person, as the determinate being of freedom. With this, Hegel takes the theory of property beyond its former state. He leaves behind its deductive theories in all their forms, as well as all attempts to derive the concept of property from a hypothesis of its original emergence in the age when the world was first peopled "by the children of Adam or Noah" (J.

Locke, *The second Treatise of Government*, edited by Th. P. Peardon, New York 1952, c. 5, No. 36, p. 22), or in regression from the state of "civilized" man to that of "the savages" as the "condition de l'homme naissant" (Rousseau, *Disc. s. l'origine de l'inegalite parmi les hommes*, bilingual French and German edition with introduction and notes, published by K. Weigand, Hamburg 1955, pp. 114, 192).

10. Already in his Jena period study of *Natural Law*, Hegel turned against the acceptance of a "bare state of nature"; it is a "fiction" and an "abstraction of man", which is introduced as a "hypothesis" "for purposes of so-called explanation of reality," in order to be able to proceed from an original unity, for which "the smallest indispensable mass of the multiplex is posited." However, such unity is, as "something not real, purely imaginary, an *ens rationis*," the "weakest unity of which the principle of multiplicity is capable"; it comes into existence in that "we think away everything that someone's obscure inkling may reckon amongst the particular and the transitory." The so-posited state of nature of man is therefore, in its separation of all "energies of the ethical sphere," "chaos" (*Natural Law*, pp. 63–64). For Hegel, what man and spirit are can first be comprehended in their ethical, historical realization (*actualitas*), where man's cultural formation has come to completion. Such formation is thus not "something purely external" to the actual being of man, as it is understood by the "idea that the state of nature is one of innocence and that there is a simplicity of manners in uncivilized peoples." Cultural formation is this actual being of man itself, and presupposes that "natural simplicity" is banished (par. 187). That holds true for right as well; in all its determinations it is based on the "free personality," the "opposite of natural determination," and "therefore a state of nature is a state of violence and wrong, of which nothing more true can be said than that it is a state to be gotten out of" (*Enz.* [1817] par. 415). Whoever imagines that man "existed historically in such primitive conditions" with "pure knowledge of God and nature" (G. W. F. Hegel, *Reason In History*, translated by Robert S. Hartman, Bobbs-Merrill, Indianapolis 1953, p. 72), "standing, so to speak, in the center of everything that we must first laboriously achieve, that is, at the core of all science and art," that person does not know "what intelligence and thinking are." Because "spirit is ἐνέργεια, ἐντελέχεια (energy, activity), which never rests," and so first finds "itself in its own labor," its concept is "not what comes first, but what is last" (*Vorlesung z. Philos. d. Weltgeschichte, Einltg.*, under the title: *Die Vernunft in der Geschichte*, edited by Hoffmeister, Hamburg 1955, pp. 161f.; see in addition the *Philosophy of Right*, pars. 18 Addition, 19.). The natural state of man is always only a state of mere possibility (see 8 above), and thus "abstract" and fundamentally incapable of becoming the basis of the theory of right, society, or state, regardless of whether it be imagined to be a "war of mutual destruction" (*Natural Law*, p. 65) or as a "primary, paradisiacal state of man" (*Reason in History*, p. 72).

11. Therefore for Hegel the Revolution of 1789 stands in an historical and objective connection with the Reformation within the history of the Christian freedom of all. After "subjective feeling and the conviction of the individual" had emerged in it, "time, since that epoch has had no other work to do than the formal imbuing of the world with this principle . . . Consequently, Law, Property, Social Morality, Government, Constitutions, etc., must be conformed to general principles, in order that

Notes

they may accord with the idea of Free Will and be Rational" (*Philosophy of History*, pp. 416–417). In this manner, the freedom of subjectivity and its realization becomes for Hegel the substance and foundation of the modern state. In recent years insight into the central position which individuality and its subjective freedom occupy in Hegel's philosophy has been regained in opposition to the idea, which in less than one century has become a stubborn prejudice, that his philosophy does violence to the individual and his freedom, and sacrifices them to the omnipotence of the state. H. Heimsoeth already pointed out in 1934 in his essay "Politik und Moral in Hegels Geschichtsphilosophie" (*Bl. f. Dt. Phil.* 8 (1934–1935), 127ff.) that "in the framework of his political thought," Hegel "was far from following the tendency to annihilate the inwardness and autonomy of the individual as a wilfulness and an intrinsic value" (145). In order to demonstrate "that Hegel's thought is decisively determined by precisely the struggle for recognition and preservation of individuality" (15), H. Schmitz has now come forward with a beautifully systematic investigation, *Hegel als Denker der Individualität* (Meisenheim/Glan 1957).

12. In the *Critique of Hegel's "Philosophy of Right"* (Cambridge University Press, Cambridge 1970), Marx considered solely the relationship in which private property stands to the state according to Hegel, and in particular, Hegel's stand on "primogeniture" (par. 306). He is critical of the fact that in the *Philosophy of Right*, "the independence of private property has diverse meanings in the spheres of private and state rights" (97 ff., 102). Hegel thus gives it a "double meaning"; it is therein revealed that he "interprets an old world view in terms of a new one" (102). In the *Paris Manuscripts of 1844* (Karl Marx, *The Economic and Philosophic Manuscripts of 1844*, International Publishers, New York 1964), private property is understood as "the perceptible expression of the fact that man becomes *objective* for himself" (138), and that "the *subjective essence* of private property . . . as activity for itself, as *subject*, as *person*—is *labor*" (128). Although it is evident that this determination is connected not only with English political economy, but with the Hegelian and Fichtian theories as well, it stands in fundamental opposition to Hegel due to the fact that, for Marx, "the nature which develops in human history—the genesis of human society—is man's *real* nature; hence nature as it develops through industry, even though in an *estranged* form, is true *anthropological* nature" (143). Thereby, for Marx, the substantial determination of man as subjectivity falls away; therefore, in the identity of human and social being, private property, as the sensuous objectification of man, is at the same time characterized by alienation, whereby it "becomes to himself a strange and inhuman object" so that "the assertion of his life is the alienation of his life, . . . his realization is his loss of reality, is an *alien* reality" (138). Whereas Hegel incorporates into the theory of property the determination of the freedom of the person from out of subjectivity, a determination which cannot be generated from the context of the being of man posited with society, Marx conceives property exclusively socially, in accord with the concept of society as the "true nature" of man.

13. See Immanuel Kant, *Metaphysical Elements of Justice* (1797), par. 22. Kant here defines "personal right of a thinglike character" through the "possession of an external object as an object of the will and the use of it as a person," and refers the

"household" back to this right. Hegel rejected the thusly grounded Kantian theory of marriage as "shameful" (*Philosophy of Right*, par. 75) in its subordination of marriage to the relation of "earning a living" (*Metaphysical Elements of Justice*, par. 23) and contract. Here it is manifest for Hegel that a theory of subjective freedom which does not get developed into a theory of its realization is fundamentally incapable of conceiving legal as well as ethical institutions. Just as Kant must introduce into marriage, through recourse to the person-object of the will relation (contract), the concept of the "object of the will" contradicting marriage's personal substance, so, on the other hand, Schlegel's romantic aesthetic theory of subjectivity reduces marriage to an element of the "caprice of bodily desire" (*Philosophy of Right*, par. 164). Where reality belongs to the freedom of subjectivity only in the form of the stuff given for its application, there one cannot succeed in conceiving the speculative nature of the substantial relationships of marriage and family as institutions.

Morality and Ethical Life: Hegel's Controversy With Kantian Ethics (1966)

I

In the *Philosophy of Right*,[1] the Kantian "standpoint of morality" is introduced after "abstract right," which is handled in the first section, as a "higher ground" of freedom in the hierarchy of "stages in the development of the Idea of the absolutely free will" (pars. 33, 105, 106)); with morality, the will comes to an explicit awareness of its identity in its reflection in itself (pars. 105,106). Earlier in the first section Hegel had specified right as the determinate being of freedom. The individual attains freedom when he becomes able to bear rights by being a "person" and, in thereby having the right of "putting his will into any and everything," relates himself to others as persons by means of objects of the will held through "possession, which is *property*—ownership." Whereas the freedom of the person entails, from the point of view of right, that everything involving "individual particularity" remain excluded from it as "a matter of indifference," the Kantian standpoint of morality allows the person, who has in right the external sphere of freedom, to be in and for himself personality in its inner subjectivity, and so allows the freedom posited with right to be "freedom of the subjective will" (par. 106).[2] Hegel's adoption of the standpoint of morality, in

starting from and passing on to right, demonstrates that his philosophy of right, as political philosophy and "political science,"
proceeds from the differentiation of legality and morality that is
fundamental for Kantian practical philosophy. Hegel makes it
the starting point and foundation of the *Philosophy of Right*. All
further determinations which he here provides derive from this
Kantian distinction: Whereas "in formal right . . . there is no
question of particular interests . . . any more than there is of the
particular motive behind my volition, of insight and intention"
(pars. 37, 106 Addition), "this question about the self-determination and motive of the will . . . enters . . . in connection with
morality" (par. 106 Addition). In contrast to the standpoint of
legality, which Hegel takes up in the form of the imperative of
right: "Be a person and respect others as persons" (par. 36),
with morality the "inner self-determination," my insight and intention within the aims of the "subjective will," and therewith
"subjective individuality," obtains its right in opposition to the
universal and in relation to the "right of the world" (par. 33).

In this manner Hegel systematically incorporates the Kantian
distinction of legality and morality within the context in which
the philosophy of right conceives the system of right as the
"realm of freedom made actual" (par. 4) and the modern state,
founded on right in the form of law, as the "substantial unity
. . . in which freedom comes into its supreme right" (par. 258).
Just as Hegel always maintains, when critically distancing himself from Kant, that Kant's philosophy is the "foundation and
point of departure of recent German philosophy," so the Kantian view of legality and morality also holds for him a decisive,
fundamental, and irrefragable significance. The individual in
his subjectivity and moral autonomy is conceived within the
state and generally within the objective relations and institutions
of society as their subject: freedom only has concrete reality in
the state insofar as "personal individuality and its particular in-

terests . . . achieve their complete development and gain explicit recognition for their right" (par. 260). Therefore, through Kant, with the principle of morality and the inner selfhood of the "person" of right that it establishes, the determination of the modern state is philosophically brought to its concept in its "prodigious strength and depth" whereby "it allows the principle of subjectivity to progress to its culmination in the extreme of self-subsistent personal particularity" (par. 260). In this way, Hegel holds fast to the Kantian view; he takes it into the philosophy of right as "political science" because with it one can first conceive what can be expressed neither in the categories of right nor in those of social being, namely that the being-for-self of subjectivity in itself belongs to the freedom posited in right of the free individual as "person" (see par. 104). Freedom exists only when man, in his inner life, in purpose, intention, and conscience, can will "that he himself shall be in everything he does" (par. 107 Addition). For Hegel, this is the insight that Kant provided. Hegel calls it the "great and sublime side" of Kant's philosophy. With it, universal recognition is granted the principle that freedom "is the last hinge on which man turns, a highest possible pinnacle, which allows nothing to be imposed upon it," and that man bow to "no authority" when it goes against his freedom. For this, Kantian philosophy has won "great popularity"; with it, it is now known "that man finds in himself an absolutely firm, unwavering centre-point," so that he "acknowledges no obligations, where his freedom is not respected" (LHP III, 459). Herein lies the "satisfying part," the "highly important point in the Kantian philosophy" and its "high standpoint"; "what self-consciousness esteems reality, law, and implicit Being, is brought back within itself" (458, 459).

Therefore, in the *Philosophy of Right*, Hegel takes the Kantian view of legality and morality as his beginning and point of departure. In the succession of stages in the development of the

Idea, in which all components incorporated in it, the "immanent self-differentiation of the concept," are "moments in the development of the Idea" (pars. 33, 31), the beginning is not something which remains behind; it becomes "sublated" in the whole in which it stands: "What is sublated is not thereby reduced to nothing . . . It still has, therefore, *in itself* the *determinateness from which it originates*"; "thus what is sublated is at the same time preserved" (SL 107). When disregard for the individual and deification of the state are ascribed to Hegel's philosophy, this ultimately rests upon a failure to conceive sublation as "preservation"; and so the state appears, as it stands at the end, as the negation and vanishing of the beginning. With Hegel, the incorporation of Kantian morality into the philosophy of right has fundamental and constitutive significance for the concepts of right and state: They are only then based upon freedom when the individual as an "I" in his subjectivity is able to remain self-identical in the self-determination of morality and conscience and when the content of all action "enshrines for me my subjectivity . . . also inasmuch as it has acquired outward existence" (par. 110). Therefore, on the basis of the modern world and the new spirit which has come into reality in the upheaval of the age, the freedom of the self in itself, the subjective "moral will," conscience—"this deepest inward solitude with oneself where everything external . . . has disappeared" (par. 136 Addition)— are fundamentally "inaccessible" to all institutions, right, state, and society; they remain what is beyond reach of every act of force. Neither state nor legislation may break in upon the sphere of subjectivity and the inner conviction grounded upon it (par. 106 Addition).[3]

This can stand as the broad, universalized formulation by Hegel of what Kant first conceptualized, in an epoch-making turn, with his differentiation of legality and morality in the determination of freedom and of law and state insofar as they are grounded upon freedom.

For Hegel, with the independence of the individual in the "right of his particularity," freedom comes into its full development and determination on the basis of the modern world and from its origins in Christianity. Hegel grasps this in general as the principle whereby the modern age separates itself from antiquity: "The right of the subject's particularity, his right to be satisfied, or in other words the right of subjective freedom, is the pivot and center of the difference between antiquity and modern times" (par. 124). Therefore, when Hegel speaks of the emergence of subjectivity and of its relation to the world of objectivity and of legal and political institutions, it remains essential for him in the Kantian sense, that it appears in distinction from them as a "second shape"; historically it supervenes concomitantly with them. In order to make that more obviously clear, Hegel points out (and he returns to this again and again) that its formation is historically distributed among different arenas. The "great form of world spirit," subjectivity, is a "principle of the North" and thereby separated from the Enlightenment, which has its location in the "West." In a famous section of his *Lectures on the History of Philosophy*, Hegel speaks of how the German people took part in the revolution in France through the philosophy of subjectivity of Kant, Fichte, and Schelling, the form "to which in Germany mind has in these latter days advanced": In Germany, the Revolution's principle "has burst forth as thought, spirit, Notion; in France, in the form of actuality" (*LHP* III, 409). In the same sense, the *Phenomenology* states that, "just as the realm of the real world passes over into the realm of faith and insight, so does absolute freedom leave its self-destroying reality and pass over into another land of self-conscious Spirit where, in this unreal world, freedom has the value of truth" (PS 363). The generation following Hegel, and above all the Hegelian Left, took this up, and understood the sympathy of German philosophy with the Revolution as an expression of the backward political relations in Germany: Because of these relations, one was deprived of the possibility of political action, and so "instead of storming out in reality," one could only participate in the Revolution "in thought," "in one's head." The interest of German philosophy in it was only the reflex, the deedless reflection "in consciousness" of what really happened in France.[4]

This separation is not the one Hegel means. What emerged as thought in Germany, in another place as well from the political revolution, is subjectivity in its subjective freedom. Thus, for Hegel, it does not build a deedless inner life next to the world of political action. Rather, in the philosophy of subjectivity's concern for the Revolution, the principle gets positively conceptualized, that where all men are free in the legal and political sense independently of class, birth, or ancestry (par. 209), they become the subjects of law and state in their subjectivity. Henceforth, state, law, society, and the objective structures and institutions have their essence in this. With the distinction between the universal and particular will, they are now determined in such a way that they have for their substance and content freedom as the freedom of subjectivity, and so are its realization. For Hegel, what began in the turn to modernity comes to fulfillment in this unity of subjectivity and objectivity: With the Reformation, in the age when others in the world were "urging their way to India, to America . . . to gain wealth and to acquire a secular dominion which shall encompass the globe," the individual came to the knowledge that subjectivity is "that which can and ought to come into possession of the Truth." There, "in the proclamation of these principles is unfurled the new, the latest standard round which peoples rally—the banner of *Free Spirit*, independent, though finding its life in the Truth, and enjoying independence only in it." Nevertheless, for Hegel, the freedom which has been absorbed into inner life is also the freedom which has made itself the foundation of the world and of the worldly kingdoms. Hence, "Time, since that epoch, has no other work to do" than informing the world with the principle of subjectivity: "Consequently Law, Property, Social Morality, Government, Constitutions, etc., must be conformed to general principles, in order that they may accord with the idea of Free Will and be Rational" (PH 414, 416). Therefore, when Hegel calls the right of the particularity of the subject to find its satisfaction the turning point and core of the difference of antiquity and the modern age, this has the fundamental and universal meaning that with it, the political and social world comes to a determination which neither antiquity nor premodern ages in general ever knew: Subjectivity in all its "primary shapes" of "love, romanticism, the quest for the eternal salvation of the individual, etc.; next come moral convictions and conscience," now "has become the universal effective principle of a new form of civilization"; henceforth it figures as the principle of society and as a moment "in the constitution of the state" (par. 124). Hegel's *Philosophy of Right* takes as its object this unity of subjectivity with the reality of society and state distinguished from it.

Nevertheless, here lies at the same time the element which forces Hegel to proceed from morality and legality to relationships which lie beyond the Kantian framework. For Hegel, its problem lies not only in the fact that Kant, with his demarcation of legality and morality, restricts right—legitimately speaking—to external actions of choice, but that he considers the sole form and reality of human conduct to be the morality, which through the demarcation, has been withdrawn into inner life and can be verified by no example from external experience. With this, the being of subjectivity, which Kant first conceived, is limited by him to inwardness in all the religious, moral, and personal relations determining it. Here lies the one-sidedness which, according to Hegel, plagues the Kantian position in all its greatness. With it, Kant cannot escape from the dualism of inner morality and the outer reality facing it. Therefore, with Kant, morality is "without execution," it remains "an ought to be."[5] The Kantian rigidifying of the distinction of inwardness and externality into a dualism of disunion has led to a detachment of philosophical ethics from the framework of legal and political theory, which emigrated from philosophy following the Kantian distinction of legality from morality. Idealism certainly does not want to resign itself to such a disunion of legality and morality. However, it has to content itself with opposing to external reality the inner morality of subjectivity in feelings or in values, that are not and only ought to be. What is ethically essential for the inner life of the free man is supposed to exist only as an ideal, and so as something beyond reality.

II

The transition from the Kantian standpoint of legality and morality to the state by way of family and civil society has the substantial significance of "sublation," in the concrete sense that right—in all parts of the system of right between the right of the person and political right—has the freedom of all as its basis only when this freedom includes the subjective will of the individual in his subjectivity.

That is the assumption under which Hegel's critique of the standpoint of morality also stands. He calls philosophical critique which only has a negative result a "sad business," an "exertion of vanity"; it only holds up one one-sided viewpoint against another and thereby becomes a matter of "polemics and factionalism" (I, 189), instead of "refuting the limitation of a shape through its own tendency towards fulfilled objectivity, whereby it is brought to its own truth." A fully formed mind can see "the positive merit in everything" (par. 268 Addition).

As much as this transition has, on the one hand, the character of "preservation," nevertheless, through it Kant's position is at the same time incorporated into relationships which lead beyond the relation of legality and morality it has posited, as well as beyond the differentiation of ethics and the theory of right which follows from it.

The separation of morality and legality, of "ethical" and "juridical" legislation, in the specification that morality is related exclusively to correspondence with the law, insofar as the idea of duty from the law is at the same time "the incentive of the action,"[6] leads Kant to the view that everything in human actions which does not rest upon inner legislation belongs, as external action, only in the sphere of right. In the *Metaphysical Elements of Justice*, therefore, not only are property, the relation of persons to one another through objects of the will, contract, acquisition, possession, etc. treated in the doctrine of right, but so is "the household society" with its marriage rights (pars. 24ff.), parental rights (par. 28), and rights of the household master (par. 30), as well as, together with the "civil condition," the state taken in the context of public law as "a system of laws for a nation—that is, a multitude of men" who "require, because they mutally influence one another, a juridical condition" (par. 43), and finally, the law of nations and world law (pars. 53ff., 62). In contrast, ethics is exclusively a "doctrine of virtue." Unlike what in ancient times was the "doctrine of ethics (philosophia moralis) in general," the "doctrine of virtue" limits itself to "one part of moral philosophy," namely to "the doctrine of those duties that do not come under external laws."[7] Practical philosophy as ethics thus has, as "philosophy of the inner legislation . . . only the moral relations of men to men" for its content (DV p. 166). The over-all division of the doctrine of ethics entails the separation of "the doctrine of virtue from the doctrine of law" in that "the concept of freedom, which is common to both [the doctrine of law and the doctrine of virtue], makes it necessary to divide duties into duties of *outer freedom* and duties of *inner freedom*"; "only" the duties of inner freedom "are ethical" (*ibid.*, p. 68).

For Hegel, family, civil society, and state also remain objects of the doctrine of right. However, they are at the same time placed under an ethical determination as structures in which freedom includes the freedom of subjectivity. Morality is thereby freed from its restriction to the duties of inner freedom and related to these institutions as its "reality" (actualitas). This occurs in the form that the transition from morality to the institutions of family, society, and state, which for Kant belong exclusively to right, is conceived as a transition to *ethical life* (*Sittlichkeit*). The ethical is introduced by Hegel in distinction from the morality (*Moralität*) of the subjective will and its "good in the abstract" as the "absolutely valid laws and institutions" (par. 144), the "ethical powers" (par. 145), "custom," "habitual practice" as the "general mode of conduct" of individuals (par. 151), "social and orderly life" (par. 170), "class" (par. 207), "corporation" (par. 253) and in summary as "institutions" (pars. 263, 265), which, comprising "the components . . . of rationality developed and actualized," "are, therefore, the firm foundation . . . of the state" and "the pillars of public freedom" (par. 265). This "existing world" of laws and institutions is ethical insofar as in it the individual is "endowed in self-consciousness with knowing and willing" and finds there the reality of his action and "its absolute foundation and the end which actuates its effort" (par. 142); in the ethical life of institutions, the individual has a subsistence "in exaltation above subjective opinion and caprice" (par. 144). Therefore, these institutions, as "objective ethical being," "are not something alien to the subject"; "on the

contrary, his spirit bears witness to them as to its own essence."
In them, the subject has the "feeling of his selfhood" and
therein "lives as in his own element that is not distinguished
from himself" (par. 147). Thus, in its transition to ethical life as
"the unity of the subjective with the objective and absolute
good," morality comes into its reality and truth in the identity of
subjective and objective (pars. 141, 141 Addition): "Subjectivity
is the ground wherein the concept of freedom is realized . . . At
the level of morality, subjectivity is still distinct from freedom,
the concept of subjectivity; but at the level of ethical life it is the
realization of the concept in a way adequate to the concept itself" (par. 152). First when individuals "belong to an actual ethical order" in fulfillment of their subjective destiny to freedom,
do they actually possess "in an ethical order . . . their own inner
universality" (par. 153).

The sublation of the standpoint of morality thus is of such a
form that Hegel goes on to custom, habitual practice, and political and social institutions in order to conceive these as the
"ethical" reality of the subjective will and its good which were
posited in morality.

This was something already so strange and unusual in Hegel's
own age that, in his notice of the plan of the *Philosophy of Right*,
he expressly points to the distinction of morality and ethical life
and its essential significance in demarcation from Kant, who
"generally prefers to use the word 'morality,'" and from the
common practice of taking "'morality' and 'ethical life' . . . as
synonyms": "'Morality' and 'ethical life' . . . are taken here in essentially different senses"; "even if 'moral' and 'ethical' meant
the same thing by derivation, that would in no way hinder them,
once they had become different words, from being used for different conceptions."[8]

What this distinction means, and what becomes of it in Hegel's
hands, is something that can be understood neither as an exten-

sion of the concept of morality nor at all as a terminological innovation. This is already argued against in the next comment, according to which Kant has made the standpoint of ethical life virtually "impossible" and "annihilated" it with his restriction of the principles of practical philosophy to morality. The distinction of "morality" and "ethical life" has fundamental significance. With it the concept of the ethical is renewed, a concept which was historically rendered "impossible" through the emergence of subjectivity in Christianity and finally in the turn to the modern age.

Hegel develops the concept of "ethical life" in its opposition to morality both historically and in general from out of the "ethical" constitution of the free life of citizens constitutive for the Greek world. Freedom here has a form in which individuals take "the substance of justice, the common weal, the general interest" to be what is essential. (*PH* 251); here too the individual will is "unfettered in the entire range of its vitality, and embodies that substantial principle [the bond of the political union] according to its particular idiosyncracy" (251). Custom and habit thus are the form "in which the Right is willed and done"; in them the individual finds a form that is "stable" in which he stands and has his own life (252). Therefore, for Hegel, the Greek polis counts as an "*ethical* community" in which man has nothing other to do than "simply follow the well-known and explicit rules of his own situation" (PR par. 150). Ethical life is thus a "whole" in which "each part is a Spirit at home" in stable equilibrium with the other parts and thus "is itself in this equilibrium with the whole" (PS 277).

All of these are determinations in which Hegel distinguishes ethical life from morality by historically contrasting ethical life to the Christian and modern world and indicating how, within its framework, individuals are united in their own wills with the universal of the good and of right; in custom, habit, and institutions they attain the reality of their own action, without knowing of the reflection of subjectivity in itself. In Greek ethical life "morality properly so called—subjective conviction and intention—has not yet manifested itself" (PH 251). It first enters with the infinite division of the subjective and objective and with the will which "has retreated within itself—into the *adytum* of cognition and conscience" (252). The Greeks, standing in their ingenuous ethical life, were therefore "objectively and not subjectively, moral," that is to say, ethical, not moral men (LHP I, 388); in the first and genuine form of their freedom, they did not yet have any conscience (PH 253).

Therefore, Hegel conceives morality, in relation to the ethical life which has not yet been called into question by subjectivity, as the principle which could only appear as "something corruptive" for ethical life. Nevertheless, at the same time it is true, systematically and historically, that in the dissolution of Greek ethical life the higher principle of "free infinite personality" stepped into history, a principle which "is precisely the pivot on which the impending world revolution turned at that time" in its dissolution of the Greek world and its ethical life (Preface). Ethical life, which does not yet know of morality, is therefore not "the highest point of view for Spiritual self-consciousness" (PH 264), so "beautiful, attractive and interesting . . . its manifestation is." It lacks the "reflection of thought within itself . . . illimitable Self-Consciousness." Therefore spirit could remain at the standpoint of the beautiful spiritual unity for only a short period. The "element . . . of subjectivity—inward morality, individual reflection, and an inner life generally," which was for Greek ethical life the source of its ruin, is therefore conceived by Hegel at the same time in positive terms as the "element in which further advance originated" (264, 265).[9]

Nevertheless, in the *Philosophy of Right*, Hegel resurrects the "standpoint of ethical life" destroyed by Kant, and thereby

harks back in its characterization to determinations that belong
to it in the Greek world, as when he points to the "ethical community" or characterizes the system of ethical determinations in
terms of "ethical powers" which stand in a "circle of necessity"
(PR pars. 150, 145). This reference to ethical life's Greek reality,
which is also systematically decisive for its concept, is given direct supporting evidence by Hegel's marginal notes to par. 151
intended for his lectures. There, in connection with the determination that the universal mode of conduct of individuals is
grounded in custom and habit, he notes down translations from
the Greek ethos: "Custom—ῆθος—the ancients know nothing of
conscience—Riemer: ἦθος ion. ἔθος—custom, use—(a superior
dwelling in the case of Herodotus) man's tradition—custom—
perhaps from "residence" [Sitte—Sitz] ? . . . mode of being and
life."[10] The reference to the Greek ethos is thus unequivocal.
Nevertheless, it has nothing to do with an idealization and glor-
ification of the Greek world which harks back to it as an original
state of grace. The positivity and world-historical significance of
morality already excludes the possibility that morality could be
understood by Hegel as a "state of decay" due to the dissolution
of ethical life following from it. He always opposed politically
and intellectually every attempt of restoration to return to antiquity. The call to it is, wherever it is raised, "the escape of an
incapacity which cannot enjoy the rich material of development
which it sees before it, and which demands to be controlled and
comprehended in its very depths by thought" (LHP I, 47–48).
Thus all restorative interpretations must be permanently set
aside.

What actually occurs in the adoption of the standpoint of ethical life is something else. With it, Hegel achieves the sublation
of the Kantian ethic, which limits itself to the inner determination of the will, by rescinding the dissolution of ethical life
consummated in this ethic, and incorporating morality into

philosophical "politics." Since the renewal of an Aristotelian practical philosophy encompassing both ethics and politics, a renewal deriving above all from Melanchthon, this philosophical politics was influential as an "academic doctrine of politics taught at the primarily Protestant universities and gymnasiums from the sixteenth through the eighteenth century: . . . without any major alterations of the ancient teaching of practical philosophy, and represented by teaching posts for political science" which were called "up until Kant's time . . . Professio Ethices vel Politices."[11]

With Aristotle, ethics is the doctrine of "ethos," taken as the constitution of individual life and action in the household and the polis, a constitution developed in custom, use, and tradition. It belongs in practical philosophy because "praxis" has reality not in the immediacy of action, but in its integration into the polis' ethical and institutional order. "Ethics" is therefore the doctrine of what is good and right, which determines the action of individuals as it is rendered universal in ethos and nomos. It is the foundation of "politics" insofar as political leadership and constitutional and legal statutes have their ground and determination (telos) in the praxis "ethically" constituted in the household and the polis.

Aristotle's practical philosophy is constructed accordingly. It begins with the foundation of human praxis (*Eth. Nic.* I), then treats as "ethics" the life of the citizen that is shaped into its universal form in custom, usage, tradition, and habit and does so in conjunction with the virtues and modes of right conduct founded herein (*Eth. Nic.* II–X), and finally, after a chapter entitled "Oekonomie" which has the household for its subject matter (*Pol.* I, 3–18), concludes itself as "Politics," addressing the established political orders in their ethical grounding.[12]

In his adoption of the standpoint of ethical life, Hegel latches on to the tradition of "politics" deriving from Aristotle. The external structure of the *Philosophy of Right* already shows this. In passing beyond a morality which is foreign to "politics," it incorporates it, in the further development of family, society, and state as shapes of "ethical life," into that doctrine belonging to "politics" which considers institutions as the reality of particular action. Thereby it passes over from the ethics of morality to the ethics of "politics," which had previously vanished with it. It takes up its tradition in latching on to scholastic philosophy and sets it in relation to contemporary reality, which has been separated from that tradition by the principle of subjectivity. Thus, in a renewal of the scholastic system preserving the Aristotelian tradition, Hegel presents the *Philosophy of Right* as a "manual" and "compendium" like the *Encyclopedia of Philosophical Sciences* (Heidelberg 1817), intended to serve the lectures which he delivered in the course of his "professional duties," and in which he gave the "requisite elucidation" to the paragraphs of the manual (see the Preface), as was the method of the Scholastics. In an 1816 letter to Friedrich v. Raumer, in which Hegel comes to grips with the then-ruling view that, in philosophy, "the determination and variety of information" is "superfluous for the Idea, and indeed contrary to it," Hegel spoke of the necessity of "forming the wide field of objects which belong in philosophy into an ordered whole built in and through its parts" (3, 319) and in this regard noted that "a few of the old sciences, logic, empirical psychology, and natural law, had still contained something of morality" (3, 318). In the Preface to the *Philosophy of Right* it is stated analogously that it is "a piece of *luck* for philosophic science" that the tradition within scholastic philosophy could continue to have influence up till the threshhold of the present age, even though it must come into "variance" with it.

Nevertheless, in Hegel's adoption of the institutional ethics belonging to "politics," this connection is neither a simple renewal nor a continuation. Practical philosophy had once before been brought to a systematic summary by Christian Wolff in his "Philosophia practica universalis" and in the "Philosophia Moralia sive Ethica," "Oeconomica" and "Philosophia civilis" subsumed under it. In it however, the ancient practical philosophy was preserved only "in thought," without any relation to the present reality. Consequently, the ethics here externally still falling under politics had to lose its connection to ethical institutions. In Wolff's dissolution of ethical life, it becomes reduced to the inner determination of human action by "human nature." Thus, in Wolff's "Philosophia practica" it still certainly remains true that it teaches the ways in which the free man can determine his actions through laws according to his nature;[13] at the same time, however, it restricts itself to the law which determines the action of the free individual in his inwardness as the law of his human nature. In this turn, "custom" loses its institutional character, which is implicitly constitutive for the ethics belonging to philosophical "politics." Wolff defines it as the "constant, ever existing way to determine (one's own) action."[14] Customs are thus, as Wolff states in opposition to those who say, "qui de moribus hominum ex instituto commentati sunt," only "mores animi." They are based exclusively upon "inner principles."[15] With this, the concept of institutional ethical life is annulled; the principle of morality, then coming into hegemony, takes its place and does so in Wolff's case, still within the framework of traditional Aristotelian practical philosophy and "politics."

What is revealed in this turn to "morality" by Wolff, is that morality, as the great world-historical principle that it is for Hegel, coming out of the final developments of scholastic philosophy, at the same time entails the dissolution of the ethical meaning of institutions: ethics is restricted to inwardness and cast of mind in such a way that no external realization corresponds to it.

This dissolution of the institutional ethics of "politics" is presupposed by Kant. In grounding ethics in morality, he makes a "new beginning," whereby he expects to see "one after another of the long-established systems collapsing like a house of cards and its hangers-on scattering" (DV 6). This beginning entails that only the "powers of the human mind" (7) remain related to the law of ethics; therefore, for Kant, custom has entirely lost its ethical meaning: "the German word *Sitten*, like the Latin *mores*, means only manners and customs" (13).

When Hegel characterizes the principles of Kant's practical philosophy as destroying and rendering impossible the standpoint of ethical life, he is dealing with this dissolution of the ethical meaning of the objective customs and institutions that, in the tradition, grounded the inherence of ethics in politics. The abstractness of morality is grounded herein, inasmuch as, in the separation and detachment of the structures of ethical life, morality does not stand as the ground and substance of political and social institutions, but has these outside itself as something external.

Hegel's *Philosophy of Right* undertakes to correct this "abstractness." To this end, it renews the institutional ethics belonging to the tradition of Aristotle's *Politics*, but does so by having it incorporate the great principle of subjectivity and morality and making it its subject. Therefore, ethical life in Hegel is no longer identical with the "ethos" of Aristotelian practical philosophy. It contains the standpoint of morality formerly distinguished from it, and thereby liberates this morality from the separation from reality deriving from the end of the tradition of politics. This reality itself has emerged, in the turning of the age, and with the political and social revolution and the grounding of law and state upon freedom, such that it has subjectivity as its subject and freedom as its substance.

III

Where ethics has action for its object only in the inner determination of the will in itself and not in the relationships of the world in which the individual lives and stands, Hegel's sublation of morality in and through objective institutions, habits, and laws must appear as a negation and challenge to the moral autonomy of the individual in the hidden motivation of his action; the concept of ethical being may seem to remain outside the horizon of ethics or else be suspected of being the instrument of a philosophical "Machiavellianism," which Hegel uses to assert political power and force as something higher than moral selfhood to allow them to triumph over the impotence of the individual.[16]

There are formulations in the *Philosophy of Right* and elsewhere in Hegel that could support such interpretations. However, even where Hegel takes an orientation reminiscent of Greek ethical life and opposes to the individual absolutely valid laws and institutions, as "ethical powers which regulate the life of individuals" "in exaltation above subjective opinion and caprice," there is always also entailed the no less fundamental determination that it is in individuals that these ethical powers "are represented, have the shape of appearance, and become actualized" as an objective "circle of necessity" (pars. 144, 145). This dual character of the relation of particular and universal is constitutive of what ethical life means as the determination of political and social institutions. The "ethical substance and its laws and powers are on the one hand over and against the subject" and his particular will, "and from his point of view they *are*— 'are' in the highest sense of self-subsistent being" with "an absolute authority and power infinitely more firmly established then the being of nature" (par. 145). At the same time, however, they are for the subject that "in which he lives as in his own element which is not distinguished from himself" (par. 147).

Objective ethical life thus consists in the "general mode of conduct" of individuals who are "identified with the actual order" (par. 151). In this sense of ethical life, the state is for Hegel "the actuality of concrete freedom," because on its basis "personal individuality and its particular interests" on the one hand "achieve their complete development and gain explicit recognition for their right" and, on the other hand, "also pass over of their own accord into the interests of the universal" (par. 260). Therefore, the relation of the particular and the universal that is fundamental to ethical life finds its highest fulfillment in that "the universal does not prevail or achieve completion except along with particular interests and through the co-operation of particular knowing and willing; and the individuals likewise do not live as private persons . . . but in the very act of willing . . . they will the universal in the light of the universal, and their activity is consciously aimed at none but the universal end" (par. 260).

Thus the "inter-penetration of the substantive and the particular" (par. 261) in their differentiation is the aspect through which Hegel differentiates ethical being and objective institutions as shapes of ethical life from the relationships of universal and particular in the Kantian standpoint of morality, for which the universal restricts itself to determining the particular will with respect to its motive through imperatives of ethical life and in a "perennial ought to be" of duty. As much as this interpenetration and unity of particular and universal belongs to Hegel's philosophy in general in its tendency to break up and render fluid the "hardfast opposition of the subjective and the objective," which it condemns as an abstraction of the understanding, it is nevertheless substantially and concretely grounded in the *Philosophy of Right* in the transition of the moral will to its manifestation as action (par. 118), insofar as action and activity are the "process of translating the subjective purpose into objectivity" and thereby of bringing the subjective will with its ends to attain "not a new one-sided character but only its realization" (pars. 8, 8 Addition).[17]

Action is thus the realization of the moral will. With this Hegel takes up the concept of praxis fundamental to Aristotelian politics and ethics. "Ethos" and "nomos" are the orders of dwelling and living grounded on custom and tradition, together with the standard of just conduct and action posited by them. Praxis is generally the mode of action specific to a type of living being and thus the mode of life in which it achieves its fulfilled existence. The practical philosophy which "gathers round man" and takes human praxis as its object, becomes ethics in the form of a theory of ethical orders and institutions. With this, however, the Aristotelian determination of praxis comes into play, such that the individual does not stand externally in his action and life, but stands in an existing world of ethical orders and institutions where his action and life come to their realization in being educated to the universal form of ethos. What potentialities and abilities man possesses by nature are realized in life and action in that these enter into the universal forms of ethical life and are educated to them. The reality of abilities and deeds is thus not the abstract immediate act in its performance, but rather the art (τέχνη) and the insight (ἐπιστήμη) grounding it. Proceeding from this premise, Aristotle states that one becomes just in the same way in which one becomes a zither player, learning and practicing the zither by playing it. Since one's own life and action integrate themselves into the ethical order and have the universal form of their realization in it, they attain virtue as the deportment of just and good conduct: "Doing what is just, we become just." Man becomes "ethical," doing what he can in a good or bad manner; his action consists and has its determinacy in the habit of the universal: "From this it is also plain that none of the moral virtues arises in us by nature: for nothing that exists by nature can form a habit contrary to its nature. For instance, the stone which by nature moves downwards cannot be habituated to move upwards, not even if one tries to train it by throwing it up ten thousand times; . . . Neither by nature, then, nor contrary to nature do the virtues arise in us; rather we are adapted by nature to receive them, and are made perfect by habit."[18]

Hegel's determination that ethical life consists in objective political and social institutions thus presupposes the Aristotelian concept of an ethical realization of human life and action. Institutions are ethical insofar as they become for individuals their habitual being and their universal mode of conduct (par. 150). Breaking through every form of reification of objectivity, Hegel takes up the ethical determination of institutions in Aristotle's sense; this entails that just as these are reality for individual action, so they consist in and only have reality in the life and action of individuals. Virtue as "deportment" in individual life and action therefore has at the same time "objective" significance: Only where it is given, do institutions also exist in a good manner; they become dead enclosures when the life of the individual can no longer find itself and realize itself within them. Ethical life is the institutional reality of human selfhood. When, therefore, subjectivity resides within itself at the standpoint of morality, and makes itself the ground and master of what is ethical, and so renders objectivity something insubstantial and unreal (pars. 140, 140 Addition), the danger exists that the moral will will subvert the institutions giving it reality. Hegel politically asserts this against the position according to which the individual seeks his freedom in distinction and separation from the universal, and opposes to the existing institutions and the "completed fabric" of the state an ought-to-be which subjectivity permits to arise from the "heart, emotion, and inspiration" and the "subjective accident of opinion and caprice." Through the fall of what is objective, this must lead to the "ruin of public order and the law of the land" (Preface). With this, however, subjectivity's own freedom of selfhood is also ultimately sacrificed; it loses its own content and reality in the fall and devaluation of the ethical order. Therefore, Hegel in a variety of ways opposes to self-enclosed subjectivity the principle that the expression of the moral is action (par. 113), that the will first becomes an actual will in "resolving" on something and "deciding itself" (par. 12). He calls a disposition which stays undecided in its "faint-heartedness," because "in willing something determinate it is engaging with finitude," a "dead" disposition, "however 'beautiful' such a disposition may be" (par. 13 Addition): "Only by resolving can a man step into actuality, however bitter to him his resolve may be. Inertia lacks the will to abandon the inward brooding which allows it to retain everything as a possibility" (par. 13 Addition). Therefore the will is not yet something complete and universal prior to its determining and the sublating of this determining; it first becomes this as a "self-mediating activity" (par. 7).

The relation of the will in itself to its objectification as action is thereby developed by Hegel in an adoption of the Aristotelian principle that "possibility is still less than actuality" (par. 13 Addition). What this means, however—namely, that the moral subjective will first attains reality in action—is not already brought to a concrete determination by the concept of action as such, but rather in Hegel's (like Aristotle's) conception of the objective and universal institutions, laws, and customs in a state founded upon freedom, as the reality of subjective freedom. They are its ethical being: "When individuals are simply identified with the actual order, ethical life (*das Sittliche*) appears as their general mode of conduct, that is, as custom (*Sitte*), while the habitual practice of ethical living appears as a second nature" which "is the soul of custom permeating it through and through, the significance and the actuality of its existence. It is mind living and present as a world" (par. 151).

Everything great is simple. Within Hegel's renewed Aristotelian theory of the ethical reality of individual life and action lies the insight that moral reflection in the inner struggle of duty and inclination—just as my being and life are not what is only inner, but also the personal and substantial world in which I stand and live—is also involved in the objective relationships and presupposes them, in that what my duty and tasks are, and what is to be done and considered just, fair, good or also not good, is indicated and laid down through the objective relations themselves. With this, Hegel asserts that man has to decide and act not in the inwardness of disposition alone, but rather in the relations in which he stands, works, lives, has interests, and takes on responsibilities and duties. In the sublation of morality into the objective ethical being, he thus sets up the conformity of the individual to the duties of the relationships to which he belongs, his rectitude, as the universal determination of ethical reality: The virtuous individual "has simply to follow the well-known and explicit rules of his own situation" (par. 150). These are the universal in an "existing ethical order." When "a complete system of ethical relations has been developed and actualized" in it, "virtue in the strict sense of the word is in place and actually appears only in exceptional circumstances or when one obligation clashes with another" (par. 150). However, the universal sphere and basis of ethical conduct is not the out-of-the-ordinary, but rather the Aristotelian mean "between an excess and a deficiency" posited in rectitude. It is, accordingly, that which, from the standpoint of morality, "often seems to be something comparatively inferior, something beyond which still higher demands must be made on oneself and others." Nevertheless, in this tendency to make the exception the rule for ethical life, there is a "craving to be something special" which "is not satisfied with what is absolute and universal." "Talk about virtue" thus "readily borders on empty rhetoric" in which its universal, rectitude, remains ignored (par. 150).

With the transition to the reality of life and action mediated in political and social institutions, that is, to the ethical being of individuals, Hegel thus extricates the duty limited to inner morality from the formal indeterminacy and abstractness of the perenially imperative, still empty Good; he liberates the individual from the "depression which as a particular subject he cannot escape in his moral reflections on what ought to be and what might be," as well as from the "indeterminate subjectivity which, never" reaches "reality or the objective determinacy of action" (par. 149). In this liberation he teaches the individual to conceive his "substantive freedom" as an existing world of ethical life (par. 149). The subjective will attains its fulfillment in the sublation of morality into ethical life: "The right of individuals to be subjectively destined to freedom is fulfilled when they belong to an actual ethical order, because their conviction of their freedom finds its truth in such an objective order, and it is in an ethical order that they are actually in possession of their own essence or their own inner universality" (par. 153).

In this manner Hegel reestablishes the standpoint of ethical life made impossible by the reduction of ethical life to morality. He takes up morality into the ethical life distinguished from it. He thereby renews the institutional ethics of Aristotelian tradition, in that he brings it, starting from the morality of subjectivity, into relation to the contemporary world and makes it the theory of that conduct realized in modern society, in the modern state, and in the institutions grounded upon its principle of freedom.

Hegel thereby, however, brings ethics at the same time back into the context of "politics." Here lies the aspect which has most stubbornly prevented the Hegelian concept of ethical life from being adopted and having influence in general. As opposed to the separation of ethics and legal philosophy introduced by Kant, the renewal of "politics" in the form of the *Philosophy of Right*'s manual of justice, proceeding as it does from abstract up through political right, signifies in general that Hegel destroyed the illusion that the existence and preservation of freedom could be grounded alone upon the morality of subjectivity in itself. The insight that subjectivity can only have reality when the political and social institutions are the reality of its action in accord with its selfhood, signifies on the one hand, that state and society presuppose the morality and sentiment of independent individuals in their readiness to make the universal their own concern: "Commonplace thinking often has the impression that force holds the state together, but in fact its only bond is the fundamental sense of order which everybody possesses" (par. 268 Addition). This just as much entails that the freedom of selfhood, of intention, and of conscience, and thus the ethical life of free individuals, can then only have existence and reality when the institutions are in conformity to them. Where they cease to have freedom as their substance and take the form where this is given up, the ethical reality of the freedom of selfhood is also undone, and what is known and willed inwardly as justice and the good can no longer be realized in life and action. Therefore the right, founded upon freedom and existing in the form of law, and the state, founded upon such right, are alone ultimately the guarantee that individuals will be able to find their free ethical being in institutions. The ethical life withdrawn into inner morality therefore only has its right where it is in the position of flight and retreat, and where what stands in reality and custom as justice and the good "cannot satisfy the will of better men," and thus "the existing world of freedom has become faithless" to them. Where the free individual can no longer find himself "in the duties there recognized," he "must try to find in the ideal world of the inner life alone the harmony which actuality has lost" (par. 138). In this flight, inner morality alone remains, but only as the impotence of subjectivity, which can no longer have any ethical reality in life and action. The individual thus has only the heroic possibility of making himself and his conscience count in collision with the unethical institutions, and so of sacrificing himself. That, however, is the virtue of exception. The reality and subsistence of a free ethical life cannot be founded upon it. Such a life requires as its condition the right which guarantees the freedom of the ethical being of individuals in the objective reality of social and political institutions.

Therefore, in Hegel's adoption of a practical philosophy encompassing ethics and politics, he has at the same time annulled the Kantian separation of virtue and law. He has incorporated morality and ethical life within the framework of the system of right and conceived this as the ground and condition of ethical life (see par. 4): Without the presupposition of right, freedom can only exist as an inner possibility, not as ethical reality. Hegel thus calls right "something sacrosanct" because it "is the embodiment of the absolute concept or of self-conscious freedom" (par. 30).

Notes

1. The *Philosophy of Right* is cited by paragraph in accord with its composition as a manual. Where the source is given as "Preface," it is always the preface to the *Philosophy of Right*.

Despite the sharp criticism which above all Johannes Hoffmeister has presented in the foreword to his edition of the *Philosophy of Right* (vol. 12 of the new critical edition, Hamburg 1955 pp. xiiff.) against the "Additions" (cited, for example, as par. 5 Addition) which Eduard Gans took from the lecture transcripts and added to the paragraphs in his edition of 1833, one could renounce using them only if there existed a critical edition of Hegel's lectures. In a conscious renewal of the scholastic form of philosophy, Hegel did offer free explanations in his lectures, elucidating the development of thought systematically summarized in the paragraphs (see the Preface). That makes the additions indispensable for the time being, even if Gans did choose them from the available material subjectively and certainly casually, without any critical examination of the relationship in which what he selected stands to Hegelian thought. The other works of Hegel are cited by the volume and page number of the Jubiläumsausgabe prepared by H. Glockner.

For Kant, the Akademieausgabe of his works has been used.

2. The theory of "abstract" (civil) right, here taken up in concise summary, is presented and elucidated more fully with its systematic presuppositions in J. Ritter, "Person and Property" [included in the present volume].

3. At a time when Hegel's *Philosophy of Right* was still hardly ever treated as the whole that it is, and the chapters dealing with internal and external sovereignty were instead taken in isolation as Hegel's political philosophy, H. Heimsoeth took up the question of the positive and independent meaning of the individual for Hegel and of the right of his particularity. See "Politik und Moral in Hegels Geschichtsphilosophie," now appearing in: *Studien zur Philosophiegeschichte* Cologne 1961, pp. 22ff.

4. For Hegel as well, Germany's participation "in thought" in the revolution stands in relation to the fact that what here emerged as "reality" in connection with the revolution was only "a form of external circumstance, and . . . a reaction against the same" (LHP III, 409); the theoretical participation in the revolution can therefore occasionally also be taken ironically: "We have commotions of every kind within us and around us, but through them all the German head quietly keeps its nightcap on and silently carries on its operations beneath it" (425).

For Marx, Engels, and Heine on the other hand, allusion to the difference between the "spiritual revolution" in Germany and the "material revolution" in France involves the "most peculiar analogies" (Heine), insofar as "in politics the Germans have *thought* what other nations have *done*" (Marx), as well as the recognition, cloaked in irony, of the universal and positive significance of the philosophical participation in the revolution. Thus Marx states that with it, "Germany has been their *theoretical conscience.*" Since "that abstract and extravagant *thinking* about the modern state . . . was possible only in Germany," the speculative philosophy of right is at the same time "the decisive negation of all previous *forms of German political and legal consciousness.*" See K. Marx, "Toward the Critique of Hegel's Philosophy of Law: Introduction," in *Writings of The Young Marx On Philosophy and Society,* edited and translated by L. D. Easton and K. H. Guddat, Doubleday, New York 1967, pp. 256, 257; H. Heine, *Zur Geschichte der Religion und Philosophie in Deutschland* (1834) *Ww.,* edited by Elster, vol. 4, p. 245. This interpretation of the relation in which speculative philosophy stands to revolution, an interpretation ultimately going back to Hegel himself, has been influential above all in the formulation Engels has given it; see *Ludwig Feuerbach and the End of Classical German Philosophy* (first appearing in *Die neue Zeit* 4, 1886, then as a reprint, Stuttgart 1888). Through the history of this interpretation one can see develop the transformations in the understanding of philosophy and its function following from Hegel.

5. Hegel's critique of the Kantian and Idealist philosophy "which raises the 'ought' to something of central importance," is presented and interpreted in a detailed and superior treatment by O. Marquard in: *Philos. Jahrb.* 72 (1964), 103–119. With this work, one debate is brought to a close. Marquard shows that Hegel's "special position over and against transcendental philosophy" is manifest in his critique of the "ought," and that thereby, the "idea of a unitary philosophy of German Idealism" is called into question (106). His thesis states that in this critique Hegel does not oppose "mere given reality" to the "ought," but rather takes up precisely the "refusal to accept the given as an instance" (109ff.) that is decisive for the theory of "ought" in Kant, Fichte, and Schelling. Hegel never denied or rejected the positive significance and right of the "ought to be." Nevertheless, he understood that with the separation of the "ought" from reality, this reality does not come into its concept in its progressive rationality. "Precisely because Kant, Fichte, and the early Schelling save the universal ends from the insecure reality with postulates and a mere "ought," they can find the universal in reality only far from real purpose and purpose only far from the real universal" (116). Hegel's transition from morality to ethical life is the corroboration of this interpretation. If Hegel's critique of the standpoint of "ought" and of morality is taken out of its context, then the notion of Hegel's immorality, of his reduction of morality to the benefit of political power, etc., must necessarily come into play, whereas Hegel himself is concerned with conceiving political reality as the reality which presupposes morality and sets it free.

6. Kant, *The Metaphysical Elements of Justice,* translated by John Ladd, Bobbs-Merrill, Indianapolis 1978, p. 19.

7. Kant, *The Doctrine of Virtue,* translated by Mary J. Gregor, University of Pennsylvania Press, Philadelphia 1964, p. 36.

8. Paragraph 33; see G.W.F. Hegel, *On Art, Religion, Philosophy,* edited by J. Glenn Gray, Harper and Row, New York, 1970, p. 83.

9. Subjectivity and morality, which on the one hand emerge world-historically

for Hegel as the "later" principle of "our modern days of culture" at the turn of
the age and in Christianity, appears to him in the Greek world as "the principle
of the destruction of Greek state-life" (LHP II, 99). Thus Plato's *Republic*, in
which Plato in the first instance presents "nothing but an interpretation of the
nature of Greek ethical life," is construed as "a particular external form of that
same Greek ethical life" by which "he thought to master this corruptive invader"
(Preface). Therein, Plato has proven "his genius . . . by the fact that the principle
on which the distinctive character of his Idea of the state turns is precisely the
pivot on which the impending world revolution turned at that time" (Preface).
Hegel's portrait of Socrates stands behind this. With him and his "divine sign,"
the aspect of subjectivity and morality enters into the Greek world, in that the
will here starts "to apply itself to itself and so to recognize its own inward nature"; "this is the beginning of a self-knowing and so of a genuine freedom"
(par. 279). In this turning inward, Hegel conceives Socrates as the figure who
belongs in history to that epoch "when what is recognized as right and good in
contemporary manners cannot satisfy the will of better men" (par. 138). "At the
time of the ruin of the Athenian democracy . . . he withdrew into himself" (par.
138 Addition). Hegel also directly calls Socrates the "Inventor of Morality" (PH
269). Therein lies his opposition to Greek ethical life; the "principle of Socrates"
thus "manifests a revolutionary aspect toward the Athenian State" (270). In his
condemnation there lies "on the one hand the aspect of unimpeachable rectitude
. . . but on the other hand, that of a deeply tragical character, inasmuch as the
Athenians had to make the discovery, that what they reprobated in Socrates had
already struck firm root among themselves" (270).

In this interpretation of Socrates and of the Platonic Republic as a defense
against the invading subjectivity, we find a systematic expression of the view that
where freedom is the principle of political and ethical life, subjectivity is already
implicitly included. For Hegel, the passing away of Greek ethical life is grounded
in this. The freedom of the subjective will belongs to the "everlasting history of
the freedom of man" (*Lectures On The History of Religion*, translated by E. B.
Spiers and J. B. Sanderson, Humanities Press, New York 1962, vol. I, p. 278).
The other aspect is the relation of Socrates to Christ and the change in world
history setting in with the latter. Yet here only a carefully restrained interpretation is possible. Hegel himself expressly opposes a theological relation of Socrates to Christ. One can certainly speak of "similar individualities" and "fates" (vol.
III, p. 86); yet there is "the human side", where "we do not occupy the Christian
standpoint, the standpoint of the true religion" (Vol. III, p. 78). The relation
thus concerns only the "outward history of Christ, which is for unbelief just what
the history of Socrates is for us" (vol. III, p. 86).

10. *Grdl. d. Ph. d. R* (edited by Hoffmeister, p. 417; compare PH 254f.

11. See Hans Maier, *Ältere deutsche Staatslehre und westliche politische Tradition* (*Recht
und Staat* H. 321), Tübingen 1966 pp. 7ff. The pre-Kantian tradition of "politics"
coming down from Aristotle, which is decisive for the problem of practical philosophy and ethics, has been opened once again to scholarly research and "torn
from an almost complete, if undeserved, oblivion" (4) by the presentation of H.

Maier; see "Die Lehre der Politik an den deutschen Universitäten vornehmlich im sechzehnten bis achtzehnten Jahrhundert" in: *Wissenschaftliche Politik*, edited by Oberndörfer, Freiburg, 1962. If today, with the new initiation of political science, uncertainty reigns concerning its name, and something like "politology" (Politologie) is beginning to be accepted, this only shows that its classical name, "politics," is virtually forgotten. Historical-scholarly research, little regarded and looked down upon on occasion as an antiquarian and idle pursuit, has here proven its indispensable function. The context within which political science stands also first becomes fully comprehensible in its systematic and objective significance in general after scholarly research has disclosed its history anew.

12. See in this regard, J. Ritter, "Zur Grundlegung der praktischen Philosophie bei Aristoteles" in: ARSP 46 (1960), 179–199; in addition K. H. Ilting, "Hegels Auseinandersetzung mit der aristotelischen Politik" in: *Philos. Jahrb.* 71 (1963), 38ff. Ilting demonstrates that since the Jena period, Hegel had established the basis upon which his political philosophy could develop, doing so through a "highly unfashionable approach to Aristotle" and by overcoming his "youthful idealization of the Greek national spirit" (47). The economics and politics of Aristotle made it possible for Hegel "to incorporate the results of political-economic investigations into his philosophical system. Hegel's attachment to scholastic philosophy belongs together with this immediate adoption of Aristotelian philosophy. For him it has the significance that, with it, the Aristotelian tradition can implicitly stand as a theory belonging to the contemporary world. Ethical life is the basic concept of practical philosophy. Its loss is the result of the process in which subjectivity set itself against existing institutions not in accord with it, something occurring before the freedom of subjectivity had politically become, together with the freedom of all, the substance of right and state. The return to Aristotle had the function of taking up the tradition of his practical philosophy in its original actuality in order to bring it into that relation to its contemporary world which is essential for it.

13. *Philos. Mor. Proleg.* par. 1.

14. *Philos. pract. univ.* II, par. 687: "Per morem intelligimus modum constantem ac perpetuum determinandi actionem."

15. *Ibid.*, par. 688: "principia interna."

16. F. Meinecke interprets the relation of morals and politics in Hegel in this manner. Since the systematic context of practical philosophy and the connection of ethics and politics constitutive for it are no longer seen, morality and politics in Hegel stand immediately opposed to one another, in Meinecke's view, in their "self-evident" departure from the concept of ethics posited by Kant. With this, "the new and monstrous" event took place, "that Machiavellianism was integrated into the framework of an idealistic world view both encompassing and supporting all ethical values . . . What here occurred was almost like the legitimation of a bastard." The persistence of ethical determinations in Hegel thus

appears as an "inconsistency": If there had not "remained a piece of the old dualistic ethics" in Hegel's "monistic-pantheistic world of thought," "he would have had to end up with a merciless naturalistic theory of power, in a reason of state which would know . . . no ethical feeling as its limit. His basic idealistic attitude, however, recoiled from it." See *Die Idee der Staatsraison in der neueren Geschichte*, Munich and Berlin 1924, pp. 435 and 446.

17. J. Derbolav points out that Hegel's consideration of Kant essentially concerns the transition to action, which Kant "paid strikingly little attention to in contrast to the ethical motivation of the will." See J. Derbolav, "Hegels Theorie der Handlung," in *Hegel-Studien* 3 (1965), 210. Derbolav stresses the "advance in the analysis of the problem of action" that is achieved with Hegel's theory, which outstrips the Kantian position (218f.). Its limit lies above all in the fact that the acting subject does not come into his rights "in face of the mediating claim of the universal *qua* world spirit." Critical consideration of this interpretation could proceed from the "ethical" concept of action in Hegel, adopted from Aristotle, with which the connection of morality and ethical life is grounded.

18. *Nicomachean Ethics* 1103a19 and following, in *The Basic Works of Aristotle*, Random House, New York 1941. The brief presentation here of Aristotle's theory of the ethical reality of human action summarizes what is discussed in its systematic presuppositions and implications in the essay on Aristotle's practical philosophy mentioned in n. 12 above. The supporting documentation for the passages from the Aristotelian ethics cited in the text can also be found there.

Hegel and the
Reformation (1968)

On June 25, 1830, in his capacity as rector of Berlin University, Hegel introduced the celebration of the third centenary of the deliverance of the Augsburg Confession to Charles V at the Augsburg Parliament, a celebration organized by the university senate. Hegel did so by delivering a speech in which he made the "occasion and reason" for the festivity the theme: With this observance, "the immortal deed" would be honored which had amounted to "the avowal and ensuring of the religious doctrine." In conformity with his position, Hegel had officially taken on this speech as an "honorary commission" and therefore (as he stated in a letter) had to "work it into a Latin flow of words." Nevertheless, it was at the same time a public avowal and enunciation of a personal position in the late hours of a life otherwise characterized by caution and the seclusion of philosophical thought, a life in which Hegel, in the "demagogical necessity" of the time, had held himself back "on the periphery, or rather outside it, without any relation to the active and causative sphere."

In the speech, Hegel based this avowal, which stands out as such an exception, upon what had happened in Augsburg. There "the noteworthy deed" had not been "achieved by an association of doctors of theology and church leaders," nor had there occurred a "disputation of scholars as a result of which the clerical authorities had then hit upon the determination of the proper teaching and obliged the community of laymen to accept this doctrine and submit themselves to it in pious obedience." The historical and spiritual significance of that day lay rather in the avowal by the princes of the German states and the mayors of the free cities of the empire that the teaching of the gospel should finally be purified of all possible wrong, and that therewith those who had earlier counted as laymen should now have the right to their own judgment in matters of faith. This inestimable freedom would then be won for all as a general principle. For Hegel, herein lay the reason for accepting the commission and undertaking the speech: "I would betray the matter of freedom which that day . . . brought for us, if I . . . were not to corroborate its possession through public witness" and speak of the freedom "which we non-theologians have won through the Augsburg Confession."

In this avowal, Hegel starts with freedom of belief considered as the freedom of man to have and to affirm as his, independently of all external conditions and presuppositions, "the relation that he has to God and God to him." This is in the first instance an historical interpretation of the Reformation; however, Hegel also takes up with it the grounds which philosophically led him to conceive the Reformation as the historical and spiritual presupposition of freedom, and thus to set it in relation to the freedom which was raised to a universal principle of right and state by the political revolution in France and the Declaration of the Rights of Man.

During his lifetime, Hegel is supposed to have thought of the days of Luther's theses-posting and of the storming of the Bastille—and to have honored them in one toast; we are not certain of the authenticity of this story, but it does bring out the fact that the connection between religious inner freedom and political freedom is essential for Hegel's philosophy. Almost of necessity, this connection must remain subject to the double contradiction that it does damage as much to the Christian, reformational freedom as to freedom's political and legal concept. Nevertheless, it has a fundamental and universal significance for Hegel: the inner religious and the political dimensions belong together in freedom; freedom loses its basis where they are opposed to and separated from one another.

Therefore, for Hegel, the Reformation is part of the world history of freedom, which begins with the Greek polis, since with it a political citizenry comes into the world, and comes to its conclusion with civil society, in which all, in their capacity as men, become free citizens. While in Greece only some were free and freedom had beside it the "hard enslavement of what is human and humane," we know that "all men are in themselves free, and that man as man is free." Hegel places Christianity within this passage from the freedom of some to the freedom of all: With Christ there first comes into the world within time's change the knowledge that man as man is free and that thus the individual in himself and as himself—as Hegel terms it, "in his subjectivity"—has infinite worth. Christian freedom is thus essentially inner freedom, the being-by-himself of the individual in his subjectivity; and in its religious core, this freedom encroaches upon all worldly relations. For Hegel, however, it is at the same time such that it is in itself opposed to all forms of the reign of bondage and servitude. Nevertheless, with Christianity, neither has "slavery immediately come to an end," nor "have governments and constitutions been organized in a rational way, let alone founded upon the principle of freedom." Therefore, for Hegel, the legal and political freedom of civil society is part of the history of Christian freedom. This has been built into the world essence "in a long and difficult labor of formation" as "the principle absorbed into the most inner region of spirit." It has now secured worldly existence with society and its rights of man. This is to begin with not without ambiguity. It might also be understood as a critique of Christianity, as saying that its religious, Christian meaning has become inessential with the political and legal realization of freedom, and that what is Christian has only the historical function of mediating the transition from the Greek freedom of some to the present freedom of all.

Opposed to this view, however, is the fact that Hegel determines the content of the political and legal freedom of the rights of man by relating it to the Reformation: He carries over into its political and legal concept connections which as such can be won neither from law nor from society and which lie outside their spheres.

Therefore Hegel does not allow religious and political freedom to collapse into an identity, but rather proceeds from their historical differentiation. He introduces the Reformation as a "second world-historical shape," which is also spatially separated from the process which led "in the West" to the formation of the modern political world: While others in the world were "urging their way to India, to America . . . to gain wealth and to acquire a secular dominion which shall encompass the globe," in Germany "a simple monk" found the certainty of belief "in spirit . . . and in the heart" as an "offering to the need for what is innermost." He has thus withdrawn belief from externality and taken it back into the inner certainty of the truth of God: The individual therefore knows now and henceforth that the "heart" and "sentient spirituality," as the "subjectivity of all men," should come into possession of the truth, while all determinations of externality fall away.

This does not mean, however, that in Hegel's view the Reformation erected only an "inner realm" in temperament and spirit. He calls Protestantism a "second world-historical shape" *because* with the freedom of subjectivity, the substance of freedom comes positively to its concept, which now becomes, with the fall of the old order, the basis of law and state. Since Hegel relates the freedom of the rights of man to the Reformation and to the Christian freedom of subjectivity, he asserts that there where man becomes free as man, all men become subjects of the political, legal, and social order as beings free in their subjectivity—religiously in their relation to God, ethically in their conscience, and with all that constitutes their selfhood.

Therefore Hegel can also immediately say that the freedom of subjectivity comes to its realization in the progress of history from the Reformation up to what now has happened in the fall of the old order. With it, there "is unfurled the new, the latest standard round which the peoples rally—the banner of Free Spirit, independent, though finding its life in the Truth, and enjoying independence only in it." The period from the Reformation up to our own time has had no other work to do but to inform the world with this principle: "Law, Property, Social Morality, Government, Constitutions, etc., must be conformed to general principles" so that they be rational and intrinsically in accord with the freedom of the individual.

In this manner, Hegel relates Christian freedom to modern society and its political revolution. This connection is not, up to this very day, something self-evident. On the one hand, there stand the theories of political and social revolution, of progress, the sociology of Auguste Comte, etc., in which Christianity is supposed to lose all actual significance and become progressively meaningless with the consummation of society. On the other hand, a Christian position has set itself no less strongly in opposition to this. For it, the modern world is but the fall and destruction of those beautiful times when Europe was still the "Christian Occident"; it therefore seeks the salvation and rescue of the Christian truth in the return to those times. Hegel has gone beyond such opposition; he conceives modern society not only as the fall, but as the fulfillment of European world history, with which first and foremost Christian freedom obtains in its universality legal and political reality. Therefore, every counsel to turn back to an old world is a flight of impotence, "the escape of an incapacity which cannot enjoy the rich material of development which it sees before it, and which demands to be controlled and comprehended in its very depths by thought."

Hegel corrects that first in the world-historical concept. With this, he takes up at the same time, however, the problem that lies in the estrangement between Christian heritage and modern society, and brings this to the fore. Already in his Bern and Frankfurt years, Hegel had acquired an intimate knowledge of political economy as developed above all in England; Steuart's *Political Science* was fully annotated by him in Bern, and in the *Philosophy of Right* he called Adam Smith the "Kepler" of industrial society. These political and economic studies became philosophically decisive for Hegel. They conveyed to him the insight that civil society could become politically a society of men per se, because in an upheaval without parallel in world history, it has *freed* itself of all previously given historical, religious, legal, and political relations and limited itself to the natural condition of man mediated through need and labor. For Hegel, this emancipation is precisely the condition whereby, on the basis of civil society, man is able because he is man to become, in the equality of human nature, the subject of law and state. With that, however, society becomes at the same time the "power of difference and division." It breaks apart the unity of man's being; it lands him in an existence which has outside itself socially everything that it is for itself in the substance of historical and personal life. In the Jena years between 1800 and 1806, Hegel had started off from this dichotomy in coming to grips with the "enlightenment of the understanding," in which "the divine" and "the beautiful" lose their basis, in that for it there is only finite and thinglike reality.

Since in this manner the beautiful turns into a "thing," the "sacred grove" into "timber," the temple into "logs and stones," and the Ideal into "fiction," the religious relation becomes reduced to an "entertainment" and "superstition," to a merely subjective feeling; it is understood to be without any connection to reality.

Later Hegel conceived this dichotomy as the mediation of all relations of man through objects of the will by society, whereby the being of man posited through society has immediately beside and outside itself what man is for himself in his subjectivity and in the historical substance of life.

For Hegel, therein lies the unsolved and improperly conceived problem that leads to the hardening estrangement and opposition of society and Christianity. Hegel had always argued against a theology that failed to convey the truth to those for whom "the entire compass of thoughts and inclinations is connected to religion like the rim of a wheel to its hub," by letting religion shrivel up "without knowledge" into a mere feeling and into a contentless exalting of the eternal. He had equally argued against historical theology: A merely historical treatment of religious doctrine sets aside its truth; just like the "accountant of a trading house," it only "keeps book and account of others' wealth." It is well known that Hegel's Berlin years were spent under the shadow of his fundamentally irrevocable break with Schleiermacher.

This critique, however, is not a critique of Christianity; it states that such theology does not penetrate the essence of the dichotomy posited with society, which takes the reified world posited with it as the only reality, and then lets itself be pushed along either into an inconceivable beyond or into feeling, in order to redeem the truth. With this, however, religion gets restricted to building "its temples and altars in the heart of the individual. In sighs and prayers he seeks for the God whom he denies to himself in intuition, because of the risk that the intellect will cognize what is intuited as a mere thing."

For Hegel, too, the point of departure was the suffering from the "ruptured condition of the age" and the "painful longing for the ensouled unity of far-off days"; never in his turn to society did he dismiss the dichotomy posited with it. He was just as conscious of the danger that society might make its world of objects of the will the sole reality of man, and he bore in mind this possibility. Nevertheless, he did inquire into the positive and rational bases of the dichotomy. He found it in the fact that with the mediation of all external relations through objects of the will, the individual was given the freedom of selfhood. Through its determination of objects of the will, society frees the relation of religion to everything that individuals are in and for themselves from ties to all forms of external mediation. Thus, in Hegel's view, the reification and determination of objects of the will posited with society form the condition that allows, on the basis of the juridical principle of freedom, the individual, in his subjectivity as a free being, to become the subject of law, state, and society.

Therefore Hegel can conceive the Lutheran certainty of belief together with everything that belongs to it—namely, the abolition of all relations of externality and bondage to them, and the retreat of the individual into himself and into the "innermost recess of the soul" and the "feeling spirituality"—as a universal and substantial determination of freedom and as the fulfillment of its legal and political meaning.

Because society restricts all external relations to relationships mediated through objects of the will, the individual maintains in the entire wealth of his religious, ethical, and personal being the right to be himself and by himself in his life. This is certainly not a philosophy which starts off from theological presuppositions and has them for its basis. It is a philosophy of a non-theologian, which proceeds within a theory of the contemporary world and society to conceive the religious relation of the individual underlying all institutions (the state, the ethical order, and the church) in light of the dichotomy posited with society. Even where Hegel takes a position critical of theology, he is always concerned with freeing it from its fixation upon the merely thing-like world and so setting it before the concept of the rational totality of human reality. What he thus affirms in proceeding from the Reformation and its "immortal deed," is therefore a universal feature of the contemporary world *and* of the religion that has become the religion of free individuals, who turn to themselves and to their own conviction with their thoughts, their prayers, and their worship of God. Hegel's philosophy is thus also an attempt to call belief back from its flight into the separation and indeterminacy of feeling, with which it seeks to save itself from society and its reality of objects of the will. The man who turns to God in himself should be brought to the knowledge that he is a man in the reality of his entire life and in his ethical, social, and political existence, and is able to be this in a situation where freedom has become the substance and foundation of society and state:

"To recognize reason as the rose in the cross of the present and thereby to enjoy the present, this is the rational insight which reconciles us to the actual, the reconciliation which philosophy affords." In the work of bringing this reconciliation to pass, philosophy, according to Hegel, at the same time takes up "the characteristic principle of Protestantism": "What Luther launched as belief in feeling and in the testimony of spirit, is the same as that which spirit strives to grasp in the concept" in order "to free itself in the present, and thereby find itself in it."